MARILEE PARRISH

GOD
CALLS YOU
Chosen,
GIRL

180
DEVOTIONS & PRAYERS
for Teens

BARBOUR
PUBLISHING

Scripture quotations marked AMP are taken from the Amplified® Bible, © 1954, 1958, 1962, 1964, 1965, 1987 by The Lockman Foundation. Used by permission.

Scripture quotations marked ESV are from The Holy Bible, English Standard Version®, copyright © 2001 by Crossway Bibles, a publishing ministry of Good News Publishers. The ESV® text has been reproduced in cooperation with and by permission of Good News Publishers. Unauthorized reproduction of this publication is prohibited. All rights reserved.

Scripture quotations marked ICB are from the International Children's Bible®. Copyright © 1986, 1988, 1999, 2015 by Thomas Nelson. Used by permission. All rights reserved.

Scripture quotations marked MSG are from *THE MESSAGE*. Copyright © by Eugene H. Peterson 1993, 1994, 1995, 1996, 2000, 2001, 2002. Used by permission of NavPress Publishing Group.

Scripture quotations marked NIV are taken from the HOLY BIBLE, NEW INTERNATIONAL VERSION®. NIV®. Copyright © 1973, 1978, 1984, 2011 by Biblica, Inc.™ Used by permission. All rights reserved worldwide.

Scripture quotations marked NLT are taken from the *Holy Bible*. New Living Translation copyright © 1996, 2004, 2015 by Tyndale House Foundation. Used by permission of Tyndale House Publishers, Inc. Carol Stream, Illinois 60188. All rights reserved.

Scripture quotations marked NLV are taken from the New Life Version copyright © 1969 and 2003 by Barbour Publishing, Inc., Uhrichsville, Ohio, 44683. All rights reserved.

Published by Barbour Publishing, Inc., 1810 Barbour Drive, Uhrichsville, Ohio 44683, www.barbourbooks.com

Our mission is to inspire the world with the life-changing message of the Bible.

Member of the
Evangelical Christian
Publishers Association

Printed in China.

INTRODUCTION

You are chosen.
You are holy.
You are dearly loved.

Find that a little hard to believe? Check out one of my all-time favorite verses: "Therefore, as God's chosen people, holy and dearly loved, clothe yourselves with compassion, kindness, humility, gentleness and patience" (Colossians 3:12 NIV).

This is the scripture I pray regularly over my own daughter. That she would know God chose her before the creation of the world (Ephesians 1:4 tells us this); that she is holy because she is wrapped in the righteousness of Jesus Christ (Isaiah 61:10 tells us that); and that she is dearly loved by God (the whole Bible tells us that!).

As we spend 180 days together getting into the Word of God, these scriptures are my prayer for you too. Take a moment right now and say this to yourself: "I am chosen, holy, and dearly loved." Say it over and over until you believe it! Write it down and ask God to reveal this truth to your heart through the power of His Holy Spirit.

I'm excited to hang out with you to help reveal this life-changing truth from God's Word!

Your friend,
MariLee

DEDICATION

Special thanks to Christian counselor Kevin Ness and Pastor Robert Gelinas from Colorado Community Church, whose godly counsel and teaching have greatly influenced my faith—and this book.

And in honor of Grammy B. Your love and obedience to God changed our family.

YOU ARE CHOSEN

*All praise to God, the Father of our Lord Jesus Christ,
who has blessed us with every spiritual blessing in the
heavenly realms because we are united with Christ.
Even before he made the world, God loved us and chose
us in Christ to be holy and without fault in his eyes.*
EPHESIANS 1:3–4 NLT

Some things just blow your mind. Thinking about how God chose us and loved us "before the creation of the world" is one of those things! But that's exactly what the Bible tells us.

In the coming days, we're going to unpack some of these amazing scriptures. But for right now, just take a look at this list that confirms the truth that God has chosen you to be His child:

- "You are a chosen people. You are royal priests, a holy nation, God's very own possession" (1 Peter 2:9 NLT).
- "You didn't choose me. I chose you. I appointed you to go and produce lasting fruit, so that the Father will give you whatever you ask for, using my name" (John 15:16 NLT).
- "Before I formed you in the womb I knew you, before you were born I set you apart" (Jeremiah 1:5 NIV).

*Lord God, Your Word says that I am chosen. I see the truth
in Your scriptures. Help me to believe it in my heart.*

THE THRONE ROOM

So let us come boldly to the throne of our gracious God. There we will receive his mercy, and we will find grace to help us when we need it most.

HEBREWS 4:16 NLT

. . . .

When Jesus became the ultimate sacrifice for us, we were given direct access to God. Before Jesus came, sin prevented us from being close to the holy and one true God. In Bible times, God chose priests to come between sinful people and Himself, offering sacrifices so that their sins could be forgiven.

Can you imagine standing in the throne room of God? Picture it: You're a little bit frightened as you look around at the magnificent palace. And before you, the way is closed. A large wall of thick curtains prevents you from going to the throne of God.

When Jesus died on the cross, that curtain was torn in two (Matthew 27:51)! Now you have direct access to God! Picture yourself walking boldly toward the throne of God just like Hebrews 4:16 says.

You are God's beloved daughter, a chosen princess!

Jesus, thank You for making a way for me to know and love God. I ask You to come and fill me with Your love and Your Spirit. I choose to follow You.

FULL ACCESS

This is a faithful and trustworthy saying:
If we died with Him, we will also live with Him;
if we endure, we will also reign with Him.
2 Timothy 2:11–12 amp

• •

Have you ever toured a castle or the White House? If you search online for Buckingham Palace, you can take multiple virtual tours online. Many guides have videoed their special tours of the palace. In every tour, you will see many halls and rooms that are roped off and locked. The public is not allowed to enter the royal family's private and personal areas. And that tends to be what most people are curious about!

As a beloved princess of God, you have access to all the private and personal areas in God's palace. Ephesians 2:6 (NLT) says, "For he raised us from the dead along with Christ and seated us with him in the heavenly realms because we are united with Christ Jesus."

You are welcomed into the royal family. You have a special seat at the dining table with your name on it. You are seated with Christ in the heavenly realms, reigning with Him.

Wow, Lord! Your Word is coming to life before my eyes.
Thank You for showing me who I really am and
giving me a seat at Your table.

A ROYAL PRIEST

You are a chosen people. You are royal priests, a holy nation,
God's very own possession. As a result, you can show
others the goodness of God, for he called you out
of the darkness into his wonderful light.

1 PETER 2:9 NLT

You may read this verse and be tempted to skip right past the part about you being chosen and God's very own, then think, *Wait, I'm a royal priest? What? Is this scripture really about me?*

The truth is you are chosen. You are God's very own possession. *And* you are a royal priest! Wow! What does that even mean? Let's take a look:

First Peter 2:5 (NLT) says, "You are living stones that God is building into his spiritual temple. What's more, you are his holy priests. Through the mediation of Jesus Christ, you offer spiritual sacrifices that please God."

Many other scriptures tell us that God chose us as His priests. Priests in the Old Testament were ministers of God who offered sacrifices for sin. But Jesus became the ultimate sacrifice, changing everything! And this is really good news for you and me! We'll learn more about that tomorrow.

Jesus, thank You for coming for us and changing everything!
Because of all You've done for me, I can belong to God.

A HOLY SACRIFICE

And so, dear brothers and sisters, I plead with you to
give your bodies to God because of all he has done for you.
Let them be a living and holy sacrifice—the kind he will
find acceptable. This is truly the way to worship him.
ROMANS 12:1 NLT

· ·

Have you heard about the curtain that was torn in two when Jesus died on the cross? Go look it up sometime in Matthew 27:50–55. It's a crazy true story! This wasn't a curtain like you have in your house today. This thing was massive and thick. It closed off the holy of holies where only the high priest was allowed to go once a year to make a sacrifice for the sins of all people.

As Jesus gave up His last breath, the curtain was torn from top to bottom. God wanted everyone to know that Jesus had now made a way for all believers to enter the holy place to come to God themselves. Jesus is the only sacrifice ever needed. Because of His death for us, all believers have access to God all the time. Now all He wants is your heart.

Lord Jesus, I give You my heart. Thank You
for Your amazing sacrifice for me!

ADOPTED AND CHOSEN

*God sent him to buy freedom for us who were slaves to
the law, so that he could adopt us as his very own children.
And because we are his children, God has sent the Spirit of his
Son into our hearts, prompting us to call out, "Abba, Father."*
GALATIANS 4:5–6 NLT

Think about all the fairy-tale movies you've ever seen. The princess lives in a castle as an heir to everything her father owns. She has everything she could ever need. The same is true with us. Galatians 4:7 (NLT) says, "Now you are no longer a slave but God's own child. And since you are his child, God has made you his heir."

The Bible tells us that we are adopted into God's family. We get to call Him Abba, which is a warm and affectionate term for "Father." We are heirs to everything our Father owns. And He made it all!

No matter what your day holds, remember who you are and whose you are. Your Father is the King of the universe, and He can do anything! Worship Him today. Greet Him with a smile. Talk about your problems, big and small. He cares and He wants to bless you with His love.

Abba, You are my loving Father. I'm so thankful to be Your child.

YOUR INHERITANCE

For his Spirit joins with our spirit to affirm that we are God's children. And since we are his children, we are his heirs. In fact, together with Christ we are heirs of God's glory.
ROMANS 8:16–17 NLT

You, beloved daughter of God, have a bright future in this life and a beautiful inheritance waiting for you in heaven. First Peter 1:4 (NIV) tells us this inheritance "can never perish, spoil or fade. This inheritance is kept in heaven for you."

Remember, when parents decide to adopt a child, they are *choosing* to become parents to a child who doesn't biologically belong to them. It is a legal process as well. When a child becomes adopted, that child has the same legal rights as biological children and becomes a legal heir.

Being adopted into God's family means that you are God's heir. Everything He has belongs to you. It's not like a fancy car that can rust or money that can be taken away. Your inheritance is safe in heaven for all eternity.

The Bible tells us that heaven is a perfect place with no more tears, no more sin, and no more pain. And God is preparing a place there for you right now (see John 14:2–6).

Heavenly Father, I'm so thankful that You made me Your child!

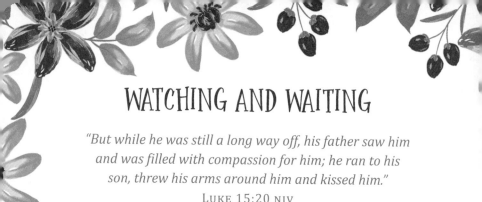

WATCHING AND WAITING

"But while he was still a long way off, his father saw him and was filled with compassion for him; he ran to his son, threw his arms around him and kissed him."
LUKE 15:20 NIV

The story of the prodigal son in the Bible is a famous one. The wealthy man's son decides to take his inheritance early and blows it. He's young and lacks wisdom to make good choices with his wealth, and he ends up completely broke. He knows the only choice he has is to run back to his dad and beg to become a servant in his home so he won't starve.

But Jesus tells us that this guy's dad was watching and waiting for him to come home. The father was full of love and compassion for his son. He welcomed him back, threw a party, and met all of his son's desperate needs and then some.

The father celebrated the return of his lost son, forgiving him completely. Jesus told us this story to show how God feels about us when we come to Him. He's your loving Father. He waits patiently for you and then blesses you with His love.

Jesus, thank You for loving me even when I don't deserve it!

EVERYTHING YOU NEED

"But I do not need the bulls from your barns or the goats from your pens. For all the animals of the forest are mine, and I own the cattle on a thousand hills."
PSALM 50:9–10 NLT

· ·

Being an heir of God isn't just about waiting for heaven. You have access to all of your Father's wealth and wisdom and goodness at all times. You simply need to ask. When you have a need, go to your Father, the King, and talk to Him about it. He promises to meet your every need.

Philippians 4:19 (NIV) says, "My God will meet all your needs according to the riches of his glory in Christ Jesus." The Amplified Bible explains it like this: "My God will liberally supply (fill until full) your every need."

Does that mean you're getting everything you want? Not really. It means that God knows you better than you know yourself and knows your every need. Talk to Him about everything you think you might want or need. He'll fill you up with all the right stuff: wisdom, healing, resources—you name it, He has it! You can trust Him to take care of your every need.

Lord, help me trust that You see me. You know everything I need. Help me sort it all out.

CHOSEN AND GIVEN AUTHORITY

But even before I was born, God chose me and called
me by his marvelous grace. Then it pleased him
to reveal his Son to me so that I would proclaim
the Good News about Jesus to the Gentiles.
GALATIANS 1:15–16 NLT

Another version of this scripture says that God "had chosen me and set me apart before I was born" (AMP). Paul was telling his readers about where he got his authority to teach and preach. And it's the same place you and I get our authority too—from God Himself!

Hold up. Did you say authority? But my dog doesn't even listen to me!

Yep, you've been given authority by God.

Just like Paul said, God chose you too. And He set you apart before you were even born! God chose you to be His child. He has called you and set you apart for a purpose. And He has given you power and authority. This week we'll take a look at what that means, what He has called you to, and how He is equipping you for that! God has amazing plans for you, girl!

God, I believe You chose me and set me apart. Show me what that
means so I can walk with You as You reveal Your plan for me.

PRIVILEGE AND RESPONSIBILITY

But to as many as did receive and welcome Him,
He gave the right [the authority, the privilege] to
become children of God, that is, to those who believe
in (adhere to, trust in, and rely on) His name.
JOHN 1:12 AMP

The Bible is full of scriptures that tell about your authority in Christ and the privileges you've been given as God's child. If you've received and welcomed Jesus into your life, then you've been given the right and the authority to become God's child. That comes with certain privileges and responsibilities. Think about it: the light of the whole world is alive inside you! So you have a responsibility to shine that light in a dark world. Matthew 5:15 (NLT) says, "No one lights a lamp and then puts it under a basket. Instead, a lamp is placed on a stand, where it gives light to everyone in the house."

You also have the amazing privilege of calling the Creator of the world your dad! At the beginning and end of every day (and 24/7 actually), you have the right and privilege to crawl up into the lap of your heavenly Father and bask in His great love for you.

I'm so glad to be Your child, Lord! Shine Your light in and through me so that others can see Your love at work in this dark world.

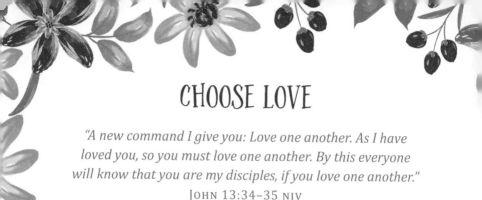

CHOOSE LOVE

"A new command I give you: Love one another. As I have loved you, so you must love one another. By this everyone will know that you are my disciples, if you love one another."
<small>JOHN 13:34–35 NIV</small>

The past several years in the United States have felt choppy and unstable as our divided nation struggled to make it through a pandemic and major political unrest. The division we've felt has trickled down into schools and churches.

Think back to the time of Jesus and His disciples. He chose twelve guys, all from very different backgrounds—one was even a political zealot!—and brought them together to show them how to love.

Jesus could have picked twelve guys who were easy to train and who did exactly what He said without causing any problems. But that's not what He did. One of the guys He chose even sold Him out to people who falsely arrested and killed Him.

The point? You're going to run into a lot of people you wouldn't necessarily choose as friends. Some you might really disagree with. But God calls you to love them anyway. Check out 1 Corinthians 13:4–13 to get a picture of what this kind of unconditional love looks like.

Lord Jesus, help me choose to love others with Your unconditional love.

AGAPE LOVE

*Love is patient, love is kind. It does not envy, it does
not boast, it is not proud. It does not dishonor others, it is
not self-seeking, it is not easily angered, it keeps no record of
wrongs. Love does not delight in evil but rejoices with the truth.
It always protects, always trusts, always hopes, always perseveres.*
1 CORINTHIANS 13:4–7 NIV

The Bible uses a few different words for love. Agape love is the unconditional love that comes from God. This agape love is the kind that moves toward people you disagree with instead of pulling away. It's the kind of love that is supernatural and always points to God Himself. It's what Jesus came to show the world.

God chose you to carry His agape love into the world too. It's not easy to love the unlovable. When you're around someone who causes you to cringe, it's time to start praying for that person—not that they would become more like you but that they would come to know the love of God. It's really hard to detest someone you're praying for. So start praying and watch how God starts pouring His unconditional love out all over you and those around you.

Lord, show me what agape love means so I can love like You do.

SET APART FOR HIS PURPOSE

"Before I formed you in the womb I knew you,
before you were born I set you apart."
JEREMIAH 1:5 NIV

You, child of God, are precious in His sight. He loves you so much and has a great purpose for your life. Check out what 1 Corinthians 15:2 (AMP) has to say: "By this faith you are saved [reborn from above—spiritually transformed, renewed, and set apart for His purpose]."

You may be wondering what your future holds. But you never have to worry. God created you with His purpose in mind. You are so special to Him. He's chosen to pour His love into you so that it spills out all over everyone you meet.

Life won't be easy—nothing of great importance ever is—but it will be a grand adventure as you allow yourself to love and be loved by God. He wants you to get to know His voice, and as you seek Him every day, He'll lead you along step by step.

Get in the habit of waking up and saying, "Good morning, Lord. I love You! What will we do together today?" And then listen for His promptings.

Lord Jesus, thanks for calling me to this great adventure with You!

FRUIT THAT LASTS

*"You didn't choose me. I chose you. I appointed you to
go and produce lasting fruit, so that the Father will
give you whatever you ask for, using my name."*
JOHN 15:16 NLT

Today's scripture is pretty clear, right? God chose you for a purpose. You were not an accident. He created you to know Him and to produce fruit. Galatians 5:22–23 (NLT) tells us a little bit more about this fruit: "The Holy Spirit produces this kind of fruit in our lives: love, joy, peace, patience, kindness, goodness, faithfulness, gentleness, and self-control."

If you look through the New Testament, Jesus has quite a bit to say about fruit. He talks about being connected to the vine. Have you ever picked a grape straight from the vine? Or picked blueberries from a bush? Or even picked some flowers from a garden? What happens after a few days? The fruit or flower starts to dry up or wilt. But if you stay connected to the vine (Jesus!), you won't wilt! You'll produce fruit that lasts and multiplies.

As the Holy Spirit fills you with fruit, those fruits overflow and bless everyone around you.

*Holy Spirit, I ask You to fill me to overflowing with
Your fruit so that it lasts and blesses others.*

TIME FOR A CHAT

Do not love this world nor the things it offers you, for when you love the world, you do not have the love of the Father in you. For the world offers only a craving for physical pleasure, a craving for everything we see, and pride in our achievements and possessions. These are not from the Father, but are from this world.
1 JOHN 2:15–16 NLT

Let's talk social media. Yes, it's time. Chances are you've had a few disagreements with your parents about your time spent online. True? If not, that's awesome! But most teens really struggle in this area and have trouble with online boundaries. One mom I know offered to give her daughter two thousand dollars if she agreed to stay off social media until she was eighteen!

Why would parents do that? Studies have been conducted and facts have been revealed that social media platforms were specifically designed to be addictive. They don't want you ever to leave or miss one single post or ad. And what starts as a harmless quest to connect with your friends and family can turn into something you never imagined, sucking more and more of your time, brain cells, and soul.

Please stay tuned even if you didn't like this devotion—check out the readings for the next few days for how to have healthy boundaries online.

Jesus, help me make wise choices online!

MORE ON SOCIAL MEDIA

If you need wisdom, ask our generous God, and he will
give it to you. He will not rebuke you for asking.
JAMES 1:5 NLT

Yesterday's devotion may have caused a physical reaction in your gut. It may have even sounded overly dramatic to you, but the truth is that more and more evil has been unleashed online in recent years.

But is social media *all* bad? Nope! God has chosen you to be a light in the dark. (And let's face it: social media can be a very dark place that has caused many teens to take their own lives!) God has chosen many to go online and share the love of Jesus! Teens and adults have given their lives to Christ because of testimonies and scripture posted online.

But using social media wisely is hard and needs accountability. Work out a plan with your parents so you don't get in a difficult place in your mind and heart. Social media can easily become an idol that takes your heart and eyes off Jesus.

Ask God—and your parents—for wisdom. He promises to give it!

God, please help me to be wise in my interactions online. I want
to be a light in a dark place. Help me keep my eyes on You.

BOUNDARIES ONLINE

Therefore put on the full armor of God, so that when the day of evil comes, you may be able to stand your ground, and after you have done everything, to stand.

EPHESIANS 6:13 NIV

Girl, it can be so hard not to lose your mind when you're online. You read a harmless post, and then there are fifty comments with people (sometimes even other Christians) arguing back and forth. Many adults can't even handle this kind of peer pressure.

But again, social media was designed to get you sucked in. Before you start interacting online, talk to Jesus about it. Ask for wisdom. Put on the armor of God. Stand for truth and love. Be a light in the dark.

If you're asking God for wisdom as you interact online, you'll begin to notice that the social media platform was designed to manipulate you. It's intended to give you FOMO (fear of missing out). And once you start to notice this, it might be a bit easier to resist. Who likes being manipulated? No thank you!

Set a time limit for how long you'll be online, and stick to it. There will always be one more video, one more cute kitty picture, one more craft, and before you know it, hours have passed. Ask a parent or trusted friend to hold you accountable with your screen time.

Lord, please cover me in Your armor as I spend time online.

24

MORE ABOUT THIS ARMOR

*Therefore, put on every piece of God's armor so you
will be able to resist the enemy in the time of evil.
Then after the battle you will still be standing firm.*
EPHESIANS 6:13 NLT

You definitely need the armor of God every time you go online, but that's not all it's for. But what is the armor of God all about anyway? Let's find out.

Ephesians 6:10–17 gives us the full picture of the armor of God. Take a minute to look it up. Now, can you picture yourself putting on this armor one piece at a time? I have often thought of this armor as heavy and clunky. It kind of felt exhausting just to put all of that on, even if only in my prayers. But Kevin Ness, a wise Christian counselor, told me that the armor of God is high-tech armor. It's not overbearing nor too much to carry. After all, Ephesians 6:13 (NIV) says, "And after you have done everything, to stand."

That changes things! Now, as I head out the door or pray powerfully for my family and friends, I suit up in the armor of God first—high-tech-style.

*Lord, thank You for this amazing armor that You've given
me to resist the enemy's attacks against me. Remind me
not to leave home (or go into cyberspace) without it!*

GOD'S ARMOR

He put on righteousness as a breastplate, and a helmet of salvation on his head; he put on garments of vengeance for clothing, and wrapped himself in zeal as a cloak.
ISAIAH 59:17 ESV

When Paul wrote about the armor of God in Ephesians, he was referring to this verse in Isaiah. The armor of God was tried and tested by Jesus Himself. He put on the breastplate of righteousness first. He knows the helmet of salvation works. Putting on God's armor before you go anywhere or do anything is a good habit to get into.

Consider sketching a picture or writing down the pieces of armor mentioned in Ephesians and taping it to your bedroom mirror. As you get dressed in the morning, imagine yourself putting on your spiritual armor too.

Talk to God as you put on His armor. Ask the Holy Spirit to remind you how each piece fits and works. After you have on the basics, don't forget to take up the shield of faith, which puts out the fiery darts of your enemy, and the sword of the Spirit, which is the Word of God. As you learn God's Word, the Holy Spirit will bring it to mind to speak clearly to you and guide you throughout your day.

Lord, help me make Your armor a priority in my wardrobe! Please remind me to put it on daily.

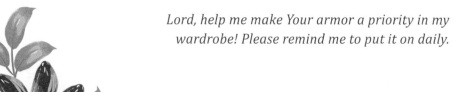

CHOSEN AND EQUIPPED

All Scripture is God-breathed and is useful for teaching, rebuking,
correcting and training in righteousness, so that the servant
of God may be thoroughly equipped for every good work.
2 Timothy 3:16–17 niv

Imagine being chosen to be on a team to play a special game during gym class but then the teacher leaves the room without telling you how to play. Oh, and if you don't figure out the rules, you fail the class and have to take it again next semester. Talk about being set up to fail!

God didn't just choose you and leave you to figure things out on your own. He wouldn't set you up like that. He has given you His Word and His Spirit to teach you everything you need to know about winning in this life and the next. God doesn't play games with you. He wants you to know Him and how to follow Him. He wants you to hear His voice.

So get into God's Word and allow the Holy Spirit to bring His words to life in you. You've been chosen and thoroughly equipped for everything God wants to do in your life.

God, I'm so thankful that You didn't leave me to
figure things out on my own. Thanks for being
with me always and giving me Your Word.

OFF-ROADING

No temptation has overtaken you except what is common to mankind. And God is faithful; he will not let you be tempted beyond what you can bear. But when you are tempted, he will also provide a way out so that you can endure it.

1 Corinthians 10:13 niv

Imagine yourself driving down the road. Suddenly you see signs that say Caution and Bridge Out. You turn around and head another direction, right?

That's kind of like this verse. Temptation comes in lots of forms. Excess dessert. Cheating. Looking at something you shouldn't. Bending the rules. Going somewhere online you're not allowed. When you're tempted and your heart starts pounding while the enemy entices you in a direction that you know is wrong, look for the signs. Pay attention. The Holy Spirit is speaking and nudging you to stay on the right road.

Girl, you've been chosen by God. He sees you. He is always with you. And He promises to give you a way out when you're tempted to do wrong. Look and listen for the warning signs when they come up.

Lord, please soften my heart to hear Your voice when I'm tempted to go off-road. Give me wisdom and strength to make the right choice.

HOW TO MAKE THE DEVIL FLEE

Submit yourselves, then, to God.
Resist the devil, and he will flee from you.
JAMES 4:7 NIV

. . . .

Did you know that you can make the devil flee? But first, the Bible says you have to submit yourself to God. Only then can you resist the devil.

Submitting to God is about obeying Him and getting in the habit of surrendering your will to God's will. For you, that might look like starting the day in prayer. You open your heart and your hands to God, and you hold everything loosely. You're willing to change your plans if you feel God leading you in a different direction. You've dressed yourself in God's armor, and you're ready for the day. You go online to do your homework, and you see an inappropriate ad on the side of the page. At first you're tempted to click on it. But then you pay attention to that Holy Spirit nudge inside of you that says, "Don't do it!" You submit yourself to God by obeying Him, and you say no to temptation. You've resisted the devil, and now he's gone. (He'll be back to try again, so don't get too comfy. But you can get your homework done in peace for now.)

Lord, I submit myself to Your will and Your plans for my
life. Help me resist the devil so he will leave me alone.

IN GOD'S PRESENCE

Because of Christ and our faith in him, we can now come boldly and confidently into God's presence.
Ephesians 3:12 nlt

. . . .

The New International Version says, "In him and through faith in him we may approach God with freedom and confidence."

Because of our trust in Jesus and all He's done for us, we get to come before God boldly, confidently, and freely. Even when you've messed up, you don't need to hang your head in shame before God. He already knows everything about you and loves you anyway. He has already paid for your sin, completely, forever.

So if you've messed up recently with temptation or screens or whatever your struggle may be, God sees you and loves you the same. Nothing you could do will ever change His mind about how much He loves you and values you.

Look to Him. Get close to Him. Share with Him what's on your heart and mind. Confess your sins and ask for help. He's the only one who knows you completely and knows exactly what you need. As you read His Word and allow the Holy Spirit to help you understand it, you'll be amazed at how much you begin to hear from God about your life.

Lord, I'm so thankful I can come to You to be restored and forgiven and fully loved.

CHRIST DWELLING IN YOUR HEART

For this reason I kneel before the Father, from whom every family in heaven and on earth derives its name. I pray that out of his glorious riches he may strengthen you with power through his Spirit in your inner being, so that Christ may dwell in your hearts through faith.
EPHESIANS 3:14–17 NIV

Jonathon grew up in church. He watched his parents serve. He learned all the Bible stories. He went to youth group and knew all the right answers. But he never let anyone have his heart. Including God.

When he graduated from high school, he let the world tell him who he was. And he went down a path that he couldn't come back from. He became a dad at age nineteen. That wasn't how he pictured his life as a brand-new adult.

Today's scripture talks about allowing Christ to dwell in your heart. You can know all the Bible stories and all the right answers, but if you don't open your heart up to Jesus and allow His Spirit to take up residence in your heart—it's all just head knowledge.

Let Jesus have your whole heart and watch as He strengthens you with power through His Spirit to navigate life on this planet victoriously.

Jesus, I open up my heart to You. Come and dwell here.

FLOURISH IN GOD'S LOVE

And I pray that you, being rooted and established in love,
may have power, together with all the Lord's holy people,
to grasp how wide and long and high and deep is the love of Christ.
Ephesians 3:17–18 niv

We do a lot of gardening around here. Last year we dug up a bunch of yucca plants. These plants have huge roots. We had to chop up some of them and experiment with transplanting them to other sections of our yard. What we found was that the giant roots of this plant sustained the shock of being transplanted. The plant flourished even when we chopped some of it off.

God wants you to be rooted like that too. Not rooted in the ground like plants, but rooted in His love. Then when life feels like it's chopping you to bits, you can still flourish in the love of Christ.

Imagine yourself with roots growing deep into the love of God. That's where your strength and joy come from no matter what life brings your way.

Lord, I want to be rooted in Your love. Lead me close to
Your heart every day. I want to experience Your love in new
and refreshing ways. Help me flourish in Your love.

EXPERIENCING LOVE

*May you experience the love of Christ, though it is too great
to understand fully. Then you will be made complete with
all the fullness of life and power that comes from God.*
EPHESIANS 3:19 NLT

- -

As you experience the love of Christ, He fills you with life and power. Remember Jonathon? He had built a wall around his heart. He didn't allow Jesus to come in and fill up his heart with love. And so he started his adult life with a God-shaped hole (that only God can fill) that he was trying to fill with all kinds of worldly pleasures. None of that worked out for him.

Many people are like Jonathon. As you meet them, pray for their hearts to soften. If you have friends who are trying to fill their God-shaped holes with pleasures, share with them how the love of God has changed your life.

God wants you to experience His love, not just know about it. Start your day with the love of Christ. Picture yourself walking and talking with Jesus as you pray. Let Him love you fully. Then you have an experience worth sharing about!

*Lord Jesus, I pray that as I experience Your love,
You would fill me with Your life and power.*

JUST IMAGINE

Now to him who is able to do immeasurably more than all we ask or imagine, according to his power that is at work within us, to him be glory in the church and in Christ Jesus throughout all generations, for ever and ever! Amen.
EPHESIANS 3:20–21 NIV

How's your imagination? Do you feel like you have a good one? God created us with the amazing ability to imagine and create. As we get older, many people tend to shut that down. But God created your imagination on purpose! He wants you to use it for His glory.

Take a look at today's scripture. It says that God is able to do immeasurably more than all we ask or imagine. Think about that for a minute. If you could imagine answering all of your prayers and deepest desires with the most perfect outcome—God can do it even better than that! Do you trust God with your prayers and deepest needs? He is good, and He loves to bless you. He may not answer everything the way you want, but that's because He has the best view of your life (from beginning to eternity!). He can do way more than you could ever think or imagine. Trust Him.

Lord, help me trust You with all my prayers and desires.

PUT YOUR NAME HERE

*For God so loved the world that he gave his one
and only Son, that whoever believes in him
shall not perish but have eternal life.*
JOHN 3:16 NIV

Although Natalie learned this verse very early in life at church, she didn't understand it was meant for her too. She thought she just needed to tell everyone else. She didn't feel loved or lovable. But she could tell others they were loved. She just didn't believe it for herself.

What about you? Do you know that you are deeply loved by God? He not only chose you, but He loves you and He likes you. For God so loved *you!*

If you've ever been on an airplane, you've heard the instruction to put on your own oxygen mask before helping others. Why is this important? If you have oxygen, you can help your family and others get theirs. If you pass out before you can get your mask on, you can't help anyone.

Basically, you can't give what you don't have. It's the same with God's love. You're chosen and loved deeply by God Himself. Lay your head on His shoulder and allow yourself to be loved by Him. Only then will you have love to spread around.

Lord, I want to know, experience, and share Your love.

WOMEN CHOSEN BY GOD

*There is no longer Jew or Gentile, slave or free, male and
female. For you are all one in Christ Jesus. And now that
you belong to Christ, you are the true children of Abraham.
You are his heirs, and God's promise to Abraham belongs to you.*
GALATIANS 3:28–29 NLT

Jesus changed everything for women. At the time that Jesus came to earth, most women were thought of as "less than" men and many even considered women to be property. They had little say in the world. Jesus talking to the Samaritan woman at the well was considered scandalous. Even the disciples were surprised that Jesus spoke to her.

But God knew what He was doing when He created women. You have an important role to play here on earth. Women were an essential part of Jesus' ministry, and several women traveled with Him. Luke 8:2–3 lists these women who traveled with Jesus: Mary Magdalene, Joanna, and Susanna.

In the coming days, we're going to talk about some amazing women God has used to change the world.

*Jesus, thank You for creating women and choosing
us to do great things. Thank You that I'm loved and
valued because You created me just as I am.*

DEBORAH, THE PROPHET AND JUDGE

Deborah, the wife of Lappidoth, was a prophet who was judging Israel at that time. She would sit under the Palm of Deborah, between Ramah and Bethel in the hill country of Ephraim, and the Israelites would go to her for judgment.
JUDGES 4:4–5 NLT

. . . .

Deborah was a prophet! She was a wise, God-fearing woman. You can check out her story in Judges 4. Deborah was also a great leader. Her people respected her. Even the military general followed her leadership.

People flocked to Deborah to hear her advice, and God set her up as a judge over all of the Jewish people, not just other women. She urged them to repent and turn back to God. She also commanded an army to go into battle, and God gave them victory.

God has great plans for you as His daughter. As you grow up, seek out God's will for you as a woman. Don't let people put you in a box if God has given you a specific vision and mission for your life. You just might be another leader like Deborah!

Lord, I submit my heart, my will, and my life to You.
Make me into all that You designed me to be.

QUEEN ESTHER

*"If you keep quiet at a time like this, deliverance and
relief for the Jews will arise from some other place,
but you and your relatives will die. Who knows if perhaps
you were made queen for just such a time as this?"*

ESTHER 4:14 NLT

. . . .

Esther is the story of an orphaned Jewish girl who became queen. Sounds like a fairy tale, right? The awesome thing is that it's a true story! God used Esther to change the heart of a king and save an entire nation of people.

The king's evil adviser Haman was determined to kill all the Jews in the kingdom. God gave Esther extraordinary courage to stand up to evil, even if it might cost her her life. She was chosen for a special time in history—"for such a time as this"—and so are you!

God made you on purpose to be alive at this period in time for a reason. As you seek Him every day, He will be with you on your own courageous journey through life. Who knows what you'll accomplish in your lifetime! God does. And He is always with you and for you!

*Lord, I believe You made me for more than I can
ever imagine. Please give me the courage and
strength to follow Your plan for my life.*

LIFE LESSONS FROM MIRIAM

*Then Miriam the prophetess, the sister of Aaron
[and Moses], took a timbrel in her hand, and all the
women followed her with timbrels and dancing.*
EXODUS 15:20 AMP

Miriam was Moses and Aaron's sister. She protected Moses when he was a baby. She grew into a leader among her people. She was known for being a musician and a prophet. The people listened to her.

In Micah 6:4 (AMP), God said, "For I brought you up from the land of Egypt and ransomed you from the house of slavery, and I sent before you Moses [to lead you], Aaron [the high priest], and Miriam [the prophetess]."

Again we see God valuing women and placing them in important roles. However, jealousy seemed to have wreaked havoc on Miriam's heart in later years. She spoke out against Moses' godly leadership and was punished for it. When she was speaking out against Moses, she was speaking out against God and His will too.

As you grow into a woman and begin using the skills and talents God has given you, remember to stay humble. God is the giver of all your gifts. Honor Him in everything you do.

*Lord, thank You for the gifts and abilities You've given me.
Help me to stay humble in my thoughts and actions.*

LYDIA, A SUCCESSFUL BUSINESSWOMAN

*A woman named Lydia, from the city of Thyatira, a dealer
in purple fabrics who was [already] a worshiper of God,
listened to us; and the Lord opened her heart to pay
attention and to respond to the things said by Paul.*
ACTS 16:14 AMP

Lydia had her own business and was very successful. She had a large home and a big household that she cared for out of her abundance. She accepted Christ as her Savior after hearing Paul speak. She became known as the very first Christian convert in Europe. Her entire household was baptized, and she opened her home for other believers to meet in.

God uses influential men and women in the business world. If God has given you special leadership abilities, allow Him to lead and grow those abilities as you get older. He can do great things with anyone who is willing to let Him lead their decisions. Maybe your entire office staff will come to know Jesus because of your leadership skills one day!

*God, help me to learn from Lydia's life. Help me to be
open and willing to share my faith with my coworkers
as I grow into the woman You've made me to be.*

PRISCILLA, THE TEAM PLAYER

Give my greetings to Priscilla and Aquila,
my co-workers in the ministry of Christ Jesus.
Romans 16:3 nlt

Priscilla was the wife of Aquila. They worked together with Paul as tentmakers and traveled with him on some of his missionary journeys. Priscilla and Aquila are mentioned in scripture as a team who worked hard together and shared the gospel with others as they went. In Acts 18:24–26, we learn about a Jew named Apollos. He was speaking in the synagogue, but he wasn't getting everything right. So Priscilla and Aquila invited him to their home and explained salvation to him.

Priscilla came alongside her husband and Paul to help them in earning a living and sharing the gospel. This was a high calling! They did so humbly as well. They could have made a big deal of telling Apollos he was wrong and making that a public debate. But they simply invited him over to their home and mentored him. There's a lot we can learn from that!

Lord, help me to be a humble team player, to work
hard alongside others when You ask me to.

BRAVE AND LOVING RUTH

But Ruth replied, "Don't ask me to leave you and turn back.
Wherever you go, I will go; wherever you live, I will live.
Your people will be my people, and your God will be my God."
RUTH 1:16 NLT

The book of Ruth is a story of God using three people who were faithful to Him during a very dark time in the world. Ruth decided to put her trust in the one true God and God blessed her because of it.

In Ruth 2:11–12 (NIV), we learn that Boaz found Ruth. He said, "I've been told all about what you have done for your mother-in-law since the death of your husband—how you left your father and mother and your homeland and came to live with a people you did not know before. May the LORD repay you for what you have done. May you be richly rewarded by the LORD, the God of Israel, under whose wings you have come to take refuge."

Life wasn't easy for Ruth, but God was with her. God used her family line throughout history, and eventually Jesus was born from their descendants!

God promises to be faithful like this too. Just like Ruth, you can trust Him no matter what.

Lord, help me trust You like Ruth did!

MARY OF NAZARETH

"I am the Lord's servant," Mary answered. "May your
word to me be fulfilled." Then the angel left her.
LUKE 1:38 NIV

You know the story of Christmas. An angel came to Mary and told her she would become the mother of our Lord and Savior, Jesus Christ. She was young. Most historians believe that Mary was a very young teenager, although the Bible doesn't say how old she was. It was customary at the time to get engaged during the early teen years, sometimes earlier.

But even at that young age, we know this about Mary: God chose her. Luke 1:30 (NIV) says, "The angel said to her, 'Do not be afraid, Mary; you have found favor with God.'"

She went through some very difficult times in her life. She was pregnant without a husband, and her fiancé planned to leave her. She probably wasn't believed when she told others the story. But God was with her. He planned for Mary's relative Elizabeth to be an encouragement to her during that hard time.

Trusting God during difficult times is necessary to carry out His plans for your life. Be on the lookout for "Elizabeths" to encourage you along the way.

Lord, help me trust that You're always with me.
Thanks for sending people to encourage me.

ELIZABETH, JOHN'S MOM

*When Elizabeth heard Mary's greeting, the baby leaped in
her womb, and Elizabeth was filled with the Holy Spirit.
In a loud voice she exclaimed: "Blessed are you among
women, and blessed is the child you will bear!"*
LUKE 1:41–42 NIV

After Mary received the news that she was going to have a baby, she
went to see her cousin Elizabeth, who was also pregnant. Elizabeth
felt her baby (who was John the Baptist) leap in her tummy, and the
Holy Spirit prompted her to encourage Mary. This must have helped
confirm everything Mary had heard from the angel.

Have you ever felt a prompting to say something nice to someone?
Don't ignore that. Many times the Holy Spirit will prompt us to encourage others at a time when they desperately need that encouragement.
Pay attention when that happens next time, and even if it might seem
awkward, go out of your way to encourage whoever God asks you to
encourage. That could be a much-needed lifeline to that person.

*Lord, help me to listen to Your Holy Spirit like Elizabeth did. I want
to be an encouragement to others. Please use me in that way.*

HANNAH

Then Hannah prayed: "My heart rejoices in the LORD! The LORD has made me strong. Now I have an answer for my enemies; I rejoice because you rescued me. No one is holy like the LORD! There is no one besides you; there is no Rock like our God."

1 SAMUEL 2:1–2 NLT

Hannah wasn't able to have children. This grieved her deeply. She begged God to give her a child, vowing to dedicate him to the Lord's service if He did so. And God heard Hannah's cries. She had a baby boy. Keeping her word, Hannah dedicated her son, Samuel, to God, and he became a minister in the tabernacle, eventually becoming a prophet and a judge over Israel.

Hannah prayed to God in worship. She praised Him for making her strong and answering her prayers. Hannah was thankful that God saw her and listened.

Hannah's life is a reminder that we can come to God about anything, knowing He sees us and hears our prayers. He is close to the brokenhearted (Psalm 34:18). If you are struggling, your thoughts and emotions are safe with God. Go to Him. Allow Him to help you sort them all out. He is with you.

Lord, I'm so glad that You are a safe place for me to share my thoughts and feelings.

ANNA, THE PROPHETESS

She, too, came up at that very moment and began praising and giving thanks to God, and continued to speak of Him to all who were looking for the redemption and deliverance of Jerusalem.
LUKE 2:38 AMP

. . . .

Anna was a very old widow who worshipped God night and day in the temple. When Mary and Joseph took baby Jesus to dedicate Him to God at the temple, Anna was there. Anna recognized Jesus as the Messiah and spread the news to "all who were looking" for redemption.

Elderly people are often overlooked or seen as "outdated" or "old-fashioned" in our culture. But they often hold a great deal of wisdom. Do you have grandparents and great-grandparents? God wants us to honor them and treat them with respect.

Take some time today and make a plan to encourage an elderly person in your life. Thank them for their wisdom and for what they have meant to you throughout your life. Continue to seek out their wisdom as you grow up. You can learn a lot from them.

Lord, thanks for my heritage and for the grandparents and great-grandparents You've given me. Help me to honor the elderly people in my life and treat them with love and respect.

MARY MAGDALENE

*Now Jesus, having risen [from death] early on the first
day of the week, appeared first to Mary Magdalene,
from whom He had cast out seven demons.*
MARK 16:9 AMP

Mary Magdalene was a follower of Jesus. He cast demons out of her, and then she went on to travel along with the disciples and other women to support Jesus' ministry. She was with Jesus when He died, and He appeared to her first after He rose from the dead.

John 20:17–18 (NIV) says, "Jesus said, 'Do not hold on to me, for I have not yet ascended to the Father. Go instead to my brothers and tell them, "I am ascending to my Father and your Father, to my God and your God." ' Mary Magdalene went to the disciples with the news: 'I have seen the Lord!' And she told them that he had said these things to her."

Mary Magdalene was the first to see and share the news of the risen Christ. She was obedient to Jesus and went to do as Jesus asked. The other Gospels confirm that Mary Magdalene was an important part of Jesus' ministry.

Jesus, I want to be an obedient follower of You just as Mary was.

LOIS AND EUNICE

I remember your genuine faith, for you share the faith that first filled your grandmother Lois and your mother, Eunice. And I know that same faith continues strong in you.
2 TIMOTHY 1:5 NLT

Lois and Eunice were women of faith in the Bible. Eunice was Timothy's mother and Lois was his grandmother. Paul took special note of their godly influence over Timothy's life and how it changed the course of his life.

In 2 Timothy 3:14–15 (NIV), Paul said to Timothy: "But as for you, continue in what you have learned and have become convinced of, because you know those from whom you learned it, and how from infancy you have known the Holy Scriptures, which are able to make you wise for salvation through faith in Christ Jesus."

Timothy's family taught him the scriptures since infancy. If you have godly family members, thank God for them. And thank them personally too. It's not easy to live a life of faith and obedience to God in our modern world. Having family members who have passed their faith on to you can make all the difference in your life.

Lord, thank You for the godly family members I have in my life and how they've taught me about You!

THE WOMAN AT THE WELL

Then, leaving her water jar, the woman went back to the town and said to the people, "Come, see a man who told me everything I ever did. Could this be the Messiah?" They came out of the town and made their way toward him.
JOHN 4:28–30 NIV

. . . .

Jews didn't speak to Samaritans. That was how things were back then. So it surprised even the disciples when Jesus was found talking to this Samaritan woman. Her reputation was tarnished. She came midday to the well probably to avoid other women who would put her down. But Jesus reached out to her. He told her that He was the source of living water.

This woman was chosen to be one of the first women to spread the gospel. She went back to her town and told everyone who would listen to come and see Jesus.

This story shows us that God can use anyone. The Samaritan woman had been married many times and was living in sin. But her meeting with Jesus had changed her. She had courage to share the good news of Jesus after meeting Him.

Lord, thank You for changing lives and hearts.
Help me not to judge others based on their past.

49

WOMEN MISSIONARIES ALL OVER THE WORLD

"For even the Son of Man came not to be served but to serve others and to give his life as a ransom for many."
MARK 10:45 NLT

God has called many women throughout history to share the gospel with people all over the world. We've talked about many women in the Bible, and now we're going to talk about some women in more recent history whom God has used to change the world.

But did you know that you can change the world right where you are too? God may put a special calling on your life to serve in a foreign land. But He often uses us right where we are the most. That means you can be a missionary in your own community. Acts 1:8 (NLT) says, "You will be my witnesses, telling people about me everywhere—in Jerusalem, throughout Judea, in Samaria, and to the ends of the earth."

One view of these scriptures is that Jesus is saying that each one should be a witness in their own family and city and then in their state and their country and finally to the entire earth. Regardless of how you interpret this verse, we are called to be witnesses of Christ where we are.

Jesus, please help me follow Your command to be a witness for You where I am.

CORRIE TEN BOOM

*"For if you forgive other people when they sin against you,
your heavenly Father will also forgive you. But if you do not
forgive others their sins, your Father will not forgive your sins."*
MATTHEW 6:14–15 NIV

. . . .

Corrie ten Boom was an author and missionary. In her younger years, she was a watchmaker like her father. Her family was arrested during the Holocaust because they hid Jews in their home during the Nazis' reign of terror. Her father died in prison. Corrie and her sister were taken to several different prisons, ending in a concentration camp where her sister died.

Corrie was released and opened a home for others who were trying to overcome the trauma they experienced during that time. She went around the world as a missionary teaching about God's love and forgiveness. She wrote many books, and her most famous book, *The Hiding Place*, became a movie.

Corrie's story is another example of this truth in Genesis 50:20 (ESV): "As for you, you meant evil against me, but God meant it for good, to bring it about that many people should be kept alive, as they are today."

God turned what the enemy meant for evil into something good.

*Lord, thank You for turning the evil that Corrie experienced
into something good that blessed the lives of many.*

ELISABETH ELLIOT

"The eternal God is your dwelling place,
and underneath are the everlasting arms."
DEUTERONOMY 33:27 ESV

Elisabeth Elliot was a missionary to Ecuador. She was also an author and a speaker. Elisabeth had a Christian radio program called *Gateway to Joy*, and she would share these words every time: "You are loved with an everlasting love, that's what the Bible says, and underneath are the everlasting arms. This is your friend, Elisabeth Elliot."

She said those things, not only because they were true, but because she had lived them. She often talked and wrote about knowing God in the midst of suffering. She knew suffering. Her young husband was murdered in the jungle trying to communicate the gospel and love of Jesus with an unreached tribe. But Elisabeth was called back to those people. She and her daughter returned to minister to the people who killed her husband.

Elisabeth was an encouragement to so many hurting people because she understood their pain. Her words of hope over the radio and in her books helped people come close to God and learn to trust Him.

Lord, I know You're with me during hard times. Please use those hard things that we go through together to bring hope to others.

LINDA STROM

"Then the King will say to those on his right, 'Come, you who are blessed by my Father; take your inheritance, the kingdom prepared for you since the creation of the world. For I was hungry and you gave me something to eat, I was thirsty and you gave me something to drink, I was a stranger and you invited me in, I needed clothes and you clothed me, I was sick and you looked after me, I was in prison and you came to visit me.' "
MATTHEW 25:34–36 NIV

• •

Linda Strom was chosen by God to go into women's prisons, even to women on death row, and share the love of Jesus with them. She cofounded a ministry to prisoners and their families. On her ministry website (discipleshipunlimited.org), Linda says, "I've loved the journey. It's always been an adventure. I am so glad the Lord invited me to join Him."

Does your church support a prison ministry anywhere? Usually there is a chaplain who ministers to local prisoners and their families. Prisoners need the love of Jesus. Maybe you and your family can pray about ways you could help support a prison ministry.

Jesus, I'm thankful You've called specific people to minister to those in prison. Please show me if there is a way my church or family can help.

TRACEE RUDD

*Sing to the LORD, all the earth; proclaim his salvation
day after day. Declare his glory among the nations,
his marvelous deeds among all peoples.*
1 CHRONICLES 16:23–24 NIV

God is using Tracee Rudd to bring hope and healing to foster kids in Colorado. Tracee had a heart for kids who were aging out of the foster system. That means there are foster kids who needed a family to love them, but they never found one, so when they turn a certain age, they have no one.

God led Tracee to a job at Colorado Kids Belong, an organization that exists to change the experience and outcomes for kids in foster care. She visits area churches to teach them about her organization and what they can do to help foster kids in need.

Tracee loves Jesus, and He is using her to make a huge difference in the lives of foster kids and families in Colorado. Today's passage in 1 Chronicles has been one of her guiding scriptures in life.

*Jesus, thank You for choosing women like Tracee to make
a difference in our world. Open my eyes to see needs in
my own community, and show me how I can help.*

INTO THE HARVEST FIELD

*Then he said to his disciples, "The harvest is plentiful
but the workers are few. Ask the Lord of the harvest,
therefore, to send out workers into his harvest field."*
Matthew 9:37–38 niv

We've been talking about women whom God has called to do specific work with special groups of people. God cares deeply for the lost, the hurting, the prisoner, and the orphan. Isn't it amazing how He calls Christians to tend to the needs of the various people groups He loves? If you've ever had a tug on your heart to go into Christian ministry, talk to someone you love and trust about it. Ask them to help you pray over this to seek God's will together.

Alex felt a call to be a missionary when he was young, and he began praying about it with his family and mentors. God opened doors for him to go to Afghanistan and share the love of Jesus there. It was and is a lot of work. He has to raise his own funds to stay in ministry in another country, but God has been faithfully leading and providing for Alex.

*Lord, if You're calling me into ministry, please help me
have the courage to follow You wherever You lead.*

WHERE IS THE JOY?

You make known to me the path of life;
in your presence there is fullness of joy;
at your right hand are pleasures forevermore.
PSALM 16:11 ESV

. . . .

There was a time in Jenna's life when she was really struggling. She loved God and spent most of her life following Him, but she had experienced a lot of sadness in her life, and the stress of grief had taken a toll on her mind and body. One day when she was journaling, she wrote, "Where is the joy?" and God answered with these words from Psalm 16: "In [the Lord's] presence there is fullness of joy." The NIV says, "You will fill me with joy in your presence." She also recalled Jesus' words from John 15:5 (NIV), "Apart from me you can do nothing."

God was reminding Jenna that looking for joy outside of Him just wasn't possible. He is the source of true joy. Allowing Him to enter into her sadness and grief is what started Jenna on the path back to joy.

Lord, I'm sorry for looking for joy outside of You. I trust that You can fill me with pure joy just by being with You!

THE HANDS AND FEET OF JESUS

Now you [collectively] are Christ's body,
and individually [you are] members of it
[each with his own special purpose and function].
1 CORINTHIANS 12:27 AMP

As God's children, we are part of His family together with all other Christ followers all over the world. If you were an only child before, now you have tons of brothers and sisters! We are also the body of Christ, the church.

After Jesus rose from the grave and went back to heaven, He sent His Spirit to live in our hearts. And we became the hands and feet of Jesus here on earth. Jesus gets His physical work done here on earth by using us. It matters what you do and how you feel and what you believe because you are God's representative here on earth. When people see you, they are experiencing God through you.

Ask Jesus to fill you up with His love and joy so that others can see His body at work in the world.

Lord, thank You that Your Spirit is alive in me.
Please fill me up with love and joy so I can be Your
hands and feet and love others like You do.

THE LOOK OF LOVE

To the church of God in Corinth, to those sanctified (set apart, made holy) in Christ Jesus, who are selected and called as saints (God's people), together with all those who in every place call on and honor the name of our Lord Jesus Christ, their Lord and ours: Grace to you and peace [inner calm and spiritual well-being] from God our Father and the Lord Jesus Christ.
1 CORINTHIANS 1:2–3 AMP

You are so special to God. God says you are set apart and made holy because of what Jesus did for you. He offers you grace and peace. And He is always looking on you with love.

Parents have a certain love look on their faces reserved just for their children. You have a special place in God's heart too. And He is the perfect parent. He is always looking at you with a special look of love. Even though there are billions of people in this world He made, you are still very special to Him.

Heavenly Father, thanks for Your great love for me. I'm thankful for all that Jesus has done for me to make me holy in Your sight.

58

MARKED

*And you also were included in Christ when you heard the
message of truth, the gospel of your salvation. When you believed,
you were marked in him with a seal, the promised Holy Spirit,
who is a deposit guaranteeing our inheritance until the redemption
of those who are God's possession—to the praise of his glory.*
EPHESIANS 1:13–14 NIV

- -

When you put your trust in Christ, God marked you as His very own.
You're His—forever! How did He do this? He sent His Holy Spirit to
live inside you. Isn't that amazing? The very spirit of God Himself is
alive in you!

The Holy Spirit is able to comfort you, teach you, lead you, speak to
you, give you good advice, help you think good thoughts, and remember
God's words. This is why Jesus said it was better for Him to leave the
earth after He rose from the dead so that the Holy Spirit could come
(John 16:7)! His Spirit can be in all of His children at the same time.

*Jesus, thank You for sending Your Spirit to live
inside me and mark me as one of Your own.
I'm so grateful for this miraculous gift!*

OUT OF THE DARK

*For he has rescued us from the kingdom of darkness
and transferred us into the Kingdom of his dear Son,
who purchased our freedom and forgave our sins.*
COLOSSIANS 1:13–14 NLT

The life of Jesus brought light to a very dark world. As a child of God, you've been rescued from darkness and transferred into the kingdom of Jesus—a kingdom full of light. God's Word tells us that the darkness can never put out the light (John 1:5). That's a promise!

Sometimes this world can still seem dark and sad. Especially if you listen to the news. But remember that you have dual citizenship in heaven! When things seem dark and gloomy here on earth, remember that your forever home is with Jesus. Things that happen here can seem big and bad. But earthly problems pass away. The light of Jesus lasts forever.

Ask Jesus to light up anything that seems dark to you, and pray that God would help you bring His powerful light into a dark world.

Thank You for Your promise that the darkness can never extinguish the light. Please fill me with Your light so I can make a difference in a dark world.

STRUGGLING WITH ANGER

*We know that our old sinful selves were crucified
with Christ so that sin might lose its power in
our lives. We are no longer slaves to sin.*
ROMANS 6:6 NLT

Have you ever struggled with your anger? Gotten really mad at someone? Maybe a brother or sister, a friend, or even your parents? Anger often happens when you feel slighted or you didn't get your way in a situation. Then your whole body gets on board with your anger. You feel it in your stomach. You feel it in your clenched jaw. You might even get a headache!

The great news is, because of Jesus, those angry feelings don't have to control your life anymore! Our old sinful self was crucified with Christ so that sin has lost its power over us.

In those situations when you're tempted to get mad, remember what Jesus did for you on the cross. Ask Him for help to calm down and fill your heart with His love instead. Allow Him to help you sort out your feelings before acting on them. You're not a slave to your feelings anymore.

God, thank You for forgiving me for the times when I've let anger take control of me. Fill me with Your love instead.

WHAT GRACE TEACHES US

*For the grace of God has appeared that offers salvation
to all people. It teaches us to say "No" to ungodliness
and worldly passions, and to live self-controlled,
upright and godly lives in this present age.*
TITUS 2:11–12 NIV

Paul mentored a guy named Titus. He was the leader of one of the churches Paul had started. Paul sent him this letter of instruction and encouragement so that Titus would mature as a leader, teaching others to grow in their faith.

This message is important for God's chosen children today too. The Amplified Bible says, "For the [remarkable, undeserved] grace of God that brings salvation has appeared to all men. It teaches us to reject ungodliness and worldly (immoral) desires."

Isn't it interesting that the Bible tells us that the *grace* of God teaches us to reject ungodliness and worldly passions? God's remarkable and undeserved grace is a teacher. Maybe that means we don't take advantage of God's grace toward us and we live in thankfulness and holiness, surrendering our desires to His will.

What is grace teaching you?

*Lord, thank You for Your amazing grace. Use it to teach and
train me. Help me learn to give grace to others too.*

THE MOUTH REFLECTS THE HEART

*Don't use foul or abusive language. Let everything
you say be good and helpful, so that your words will
be an encouragement to those who hear them.*
EPHESIANS 4:29 NLT

Whew! You can hardly go to the grocery store these days without getting an earful of foul language. It's everywhere. But the Bible says don't do it. Want to know why? Check out this verse: "A good man brings good things out of the good stored up in his heart, and an evil man brings evil things out of the evil stored up in his heart. For the mouth speaks what the heart is full of" (Luke 6:45 NIV).

Do you see what God's Word is saying here? What's inside the heart of someone who uses bad language? "The mouth speaks what the heart is full of."

So what's your heart full of? If you find yourself wanting to say something bad the next time you stub your toe or have a bad day, ask Jesus to reveal what's in your heart. Let Him pull out any bad weeds that might be growing there and fill you with His love and grace instead.

*Lord, please pull out any nasty weeds in my heart.
I want my mouth to reflect love and grace.*

FILLED UP AND OVERFLOWING

I pray that God, the source of hope, will fill you completely with joy and peace because you trust in him. Then you will overflow with confident hope through the power of the Holy Spirit.
ROMANS 15:13 NLT

. . . .

The Holy Spirit fills our hearts with the love of God. And that same power is what gives us hope. Colossians 1:27 (NLT) says, "For God wanted them to know that the riches and glory of Christ are for you Gentiles, too. And this is the secret: Christ lives in you. This gives you assurance of sharing his glory."

Christ lives in you! His Spirit is alive and at work in you at every moment! Think about this: When you fill a cup up with water to the very top, what happens if you jiggle the glass a little? It overflows and spills out! The Holy Spirit wants to fill you up just like that, so that you overflow with love and hope—and then you can sprinkle a little of that on everyone around you.

God, You are the source of my hope! Please fill me up to the top with love, joy, and peace so that I can sprinkle Your love all around me.

TALKING WITH JESUS

Jesus looked at them intently and said, "Humanly speaking,
it is impossible. But with God everything is possible."
MATTHEW 19:26 NLT

Jesus wants to talk to you every single day. Can you hear Him? Remember the scriptures we've read about Jesus wanting us to hear His voice? Sometimes it helps to picture Jesus in your mind while you pray. After all, God created your imagination for a reason! Christian missionary reports out of the Middle East have stated that Jesus is showing up in people's dreams who have never even heard of Him before. That seems impossible, but nothing is impossible with God!

Jesus is a very personal God. He wants to be your friend and your trusted counselor. He wants you to come to Him first for advice.

What do you need advice about today? Ask Jesus for help and guidance. Talk to Him like you would your best friend. You can talk to Him out loud, you can pray in your heart and mind, and it's also very helpful to write down your prayers so you can have a reminder of how God answers you!

Jesus, thanks for creating my imagination so I can see and
hear from You! I believe You can do the impossible!

THE LIFE YOU'VE BEEN GIVEN

*Only, let each one live the life which the Lord has assigned him,
and to which God has called him [for each person is unique and is
accountable for his choices and conduct, let him walk in this way].*
1 CORINTHIANS 7:17 AMP

Some of the Corinthians were becoming followers of Jesus and then making huge changes without being led to make those changes by God. For example, some spouses were ready to leave their unbelieving spouse. But that's not what God says to do. Paul tells the people to stay in their marriages and continue as before. You can share the message of Jesus right where you are, in the family you're in, in the job you have. That doesn't mean you can't hope for or make changes in the future. Just make sure to seek God's will before doing so.

God made you exactly the way He wanted you to be for a reason, and He put you where you are right now for a purpose. God wants you to be content with the life He has given you and not wish for someone else's.

*Lord, help me to embrace the life that You gave
me and share Your love right where I am.*

66

WHAT'S GOING TO HAPPEN?

*"My Father's house has many rooms; if that were not so, would I
have told you that I am going there to prepare a place for you?
And if I go and prepare a place for you, I will come back and
take you to be with me that you also may be where I am."*
JOHN 14:2–3 NIV

- -

Pastor Robert Gelinas of Colorado Community Church in Aurora,
Colorado, gave a sermon recently in which he mentioned the plan
for the future of all believers. Many people are nervous and worried
about the state of our country and the world as a whole. But Pastor
Robert reminded us of what Jesus said here in John 14. You don't need
to worry about the future! Why? Because Jesus is preparing a place
for you, chosen one. He's coming back to get you. And when He does,
"every knee should bow, in heaven and on earth and under the earth,
and every tongue acknowledge that Jesus Christ is Lord, to the glory
of God the Father" (Philippians 2:10–11 NIV).

Jesus is coming back to make all things new (Revelation 21:5),
so there is no need to be afraid. God is with you and for you, and He
always keeps His promises.

*Jesus, I'm so thankful You're making a place for me
in heaven and coming back to take me with You!*

IN HIS IMAGE

*So God created man in His own image, in the
image and likeness of God He created him;
male and female He created them.*
GENESIS 1:27 AMP

The book of Genesis tells us that we are created in the image of God. Human life is special and honored above every other living thing because each of us bears the mark of our Creator God. Just like a valuable piece of artwork, every human being is special because of who made us. We are God's creation. It's so important to remember as you grow up that every human life has value because every human is made in the image of God.

When you meet someone new, don't judge that person by their outward appearance. Their hair, shoes, and clothes don't make them who they are inside. They are God's precious creation no matter what they look like on the outside. Get in the habit of seeing other people as God's precious works of art. Even if they don't see it or believe it, you know it's true. This will begin to change how you treat everyone around you!

*Lord, help me to treat other people like the valuable treasures
they really are. We are all Your precious masterpieces.*

THE SAME GOD

But the LORD made the earth by his power, and he preserves it by his wisdom. With his own understanding he stretched out the heavens. When he speaks in the thunder, the heavens roar with rain. He causes the clouds to rise over the earth. He sends the lightning with the rain and releases the wind from his storehouses.
JEREMIAH 10:12–13 NLT

. . . .

The God who loves and cares about you is the same God who stretched out the heavens. The God who knows your name and the number of hairs on your head is the same God who speaks in the thunder and releases the wind from His storehouse.

God is always speaking love to you. Just look out at creation. The grass is a beautiful green carpet designed by God. The birds and the flowers all announce His existence. The person next to you is a miracle, woven together by God.

When you think about God's unlimited power and His love for you, what happens to your problems? Do you trust that God can handle anything you have going on?

You are the same God who speaks water into existence, so I know You can take care of anything that comes my way. Thank You, God!

WHAT OTHERS THINK

We serve God whether people honor us or despise us,
whether they slander us or praise us. We are
honest, but they call us impostors.
2 CORINTHIANS 6:8 NLT

Some people say they don't care what other people think of them, but if you take a deep look at your heart, what people say can matter a little too much. It's that whole "sticks and stones" thing. It's just not true. Words can hurt.

Do you find yourself worrying about what others are saying and thinking about you? Here's the thing: when God's power is at work in you, you can be confident in who you are as His child no matter what anyone else thinks.

When others say hurtful things about you, it can definitely sting. But as you bring those hurts to Jesus, He reminds you of the truth. You are a dearly loved daughter of the King of kings! You have access to all of God's power. You can walk right up to God because of how loved you are.

Lord, thank You for reminding me of who I am.
I never have to worry about what other people
of me, because I'm Your beloved child.

IDOLS

Among the gods there is none like you, Lord; no deeds can compare with yours. All the nations you have made will come and worship before you, Lord; they will bring glory to your name. For you are great and do marvelous deeds; you alone are God.
Psalm 86:8–10 niv

. . . .

In ancient times, the people worshipped many gods and idols. The Hebrew people knew that there was only one true God. People still worship various gods and idols other than the one true God today too. There are various religions in the world, but Americans tend to have all kinds of little idols (think smartphones, screens, social media, etc.) they worship. An idol is anything that consumes someone's time and energy more than God.

If you're struggling here, repent. Turn back to Jesus and allow Him to fill you with His life-giving light and love again.

The time you spend with God will accomplish more than anything else you could ever do. There is no one else who can do what God can do. Don't let anything take the place of God in your life.

God of all creation, there is no one like You. Fill me again with Your life and light. Help me turn away from things that suck too much of my time and life away.

71

THE GARDEN OF YOUR HEART

Do not be deceived: God cannot be mocked.
A man reaps what he sows.
GALATIANS 6:7 NIV

Have you ever grown a garden? Some people have a knack for it and really enjoy planting things and watching them grow. Jesus liked to use gardening illustrations in the Bible to help people understand what He was teaching. Many people in the crowds following Him were farmers and gardeners.

This verse in Galatians is a truth to remember for a lifetime. It's the law of sowing and reaping. The law of sowing and reaping means that what you plant is what you harvest. It's true in the natural world and it's true in the spiritual world. If you plant pumpkins, you'll harvest pumpkins. If you plant doubt and worry in your heart, that's exactly what will grow.

Your heart matters to God, and He wants to plant really good things there. If you have weeds growing in your heart, go to the master gardener, Jesus, and ask for His help.

Jesus, I ask You to prepare the soil of my heart for the
good things You want to plant there. Pluck out the
weeds and help me sow good plants instead.

FAITHFUL IN THE BATTLE

The Lord is faithful, and he will strengthen
you and protect you from the evil one.
2 THESSALONIANS 3:3 NIV

. . . .

Michaela was struggling. Every time she went online to do her homework, tempting ads would come up and entice her away from what she had to do. At first she ignored them. Then she gave in. She felt bad about getting lured away, but she kept clicking on them. One day she got caught by her parents. She was actually kind of glad. She found herself not feeling strong enough to handle the temptation.

With the help of her parents, Michaela made a plan. She confessed her sin to God and her parents. She had some consequences, of course. But she also prayed and came up with ideas to strengthen her faith and trust that God would help her resist temptation.

Michaela learned to submit herself to God first, resisting the devil and making him flee. She also learned to put her spiritual armor on. And she learned some scripture verses to say in the middle of temptation like 1 Corinthians 10:13. She began to look for the way out that God always gave her.

Lord, please help me hide Your Word in my heart
that I might not sin against You (Psalm 119:11).
Thanks for always being faithful to me!

WE NEED EACH OTHER

And let us consider how we may spur one another on toward love and good deeds, not giving up meeting together, as some are in the habit of doing, but encouraging one another— and all the more as you see the Day approaching.
HEBREWS 10:24–25 NIV

Bad days happen. And on those bad days, it can sometimes be easy to forget who you are and whose you are! That's why we need each other.

You need friends and mentors who will always remind you that you are loved and chosen by God for such a time as this. If you don't have someone in your life like that, pray that God will provide someone! I believe this is a prayer that God loves to answer. Ask Him to send you someone who can encourage you in your faith and who you can encourage too.

Be on the lookout for how God wants to answer this prayer. Friends might show up in unusual places! And remember, if you want good and loving friends, *be* a good and loving friend.

Lord, I'm praying now that You would bring someone into my life who will encourage me in my relationship with You. Let us pray for each other and help one another grow closer to You.

YOUTH GROUP

*So encourage each other and build each
other up, just as you are already doing.*
1 THESSALONIANS 5:11 NLT

Emily loved her youth group. She couldn't wait to get there every Wednesday night. After a year or two of searching, she had finally found a place to belong. Her youth pastor loved Jesus, and he taught truth from God's Word. They played a couple of games. They spent time worshipping Jesus as a group in song, and many of the students played instruments to help lead. They split into small groups after the worship time and message to discuss things with a leader and other girls her age. They prayed and shared. She was so happy to be a part of youth group.

Getting together with other believers to learn about God and worship together is very important. If this is something missing in your life, talk to God about it. It might take awhile and a few visits to various places to find the right fit, but there is a place for you in the body of believers to encourage and be encouraged.

*Jesus, please help me find a place to belong where
I can be encouraged and grow in my faith.*

TROUBLE

*Now if we are children, then we are heirs—heirs of
God and co-heirs with Christ, if indeed we share in his
sufferings in order that we may also share in his glory.*
ROMANS 8:17 NIV

- -

This world can be rather troubling at times. It's not our true home. Philippians 3:20 (NLT) reminds us, "We are citizens of heaven, where the Lord Jesus Christ lives. And we are eagerly waiting for him to return as our Savior."

Jesus Himself told us we're going to have trouble here, so we should expect some days to be hard. But He also said, "Take heart! I have overcome the world" (John 16:33 NIV).

So how can we live with joy in our hearts while we're expecting trouble? Well, we wake up each morning expecting some challenges, and we ask God to help us through each and every one. That doesn't mean we're grumpy or negative, though. Always look at trouble as a challenge that can be overcome with the power of Christ.

Life is an adventure full of good times and bad. We can find Christ in each moment, and He will give us joy in His presence!

*Jesus, I'm expecting some adventures and challenges today,
and I know You will be with me through them all.*

FAMILY LIFE

Most important of all, continue to show deep love for each other, for love covers a multitude of sins. Cheerfully share your home with those who need a meal or a place to stay. God has given each of you a gift from his great variety of spiritual gifts. Use them well to serve one another.
1 PETER 4:8–10 NLT

God has good plans and purposes for His family. He wants us to love each other deeply. And like a good parent, He wants us to share. He's given each of us special gifts to serve others and honor Him.

Think of a mom with her toddler children. She teaches them to share and treat each other with kindness and love. But sometimes those little ones go rogue. Mom has to intervene before mutiny ensues. She lovingly gets them back in order.

Sometimes this happens in the body of believers too. We don't always agree. We get selfish. We don't want to serve others. When that happens, we are reminded to love one another deeply. That love helps us give each other grace so we can get back to the family life God has intended for us.

Lord, help me learn to love others well. More like You do. Show me how to use my gifts to serve and love.

GETTING THE FAMILY TOGETHER

Let the message about Christ, in all its richness,
fill your lives. Teach and counsel each other with all
the wisdom he gives. Sing psalms and hymns and
spiritual songs to God with thankful hearts.
COLOSSIANS 3:16 NLT

When "the family" gets together, God has a plan. We're talking about the family of God again. God's given you the family you were born into, but you've also been adopted into the family of God. That means you have Christian brothers and sisters all over the earth!

And when you get together with those brothers and sisters in Christ, God wants that to be a time of encouragement and worship. It's important to teach and counsel each other from God's Word. Get into His Word together with other believers and talk about it. The Holy Spirit will lead you and make sure you're on the right track.

Being part of a healthy, Bible-believing church is really important. Ask God's Spirit to lead you to a good place to be a part of His family. If your parents already go to church, great! If not, ask God to start working on their hearts.

Lord, thank You for Your family! I'm so thankful that I have
tons of brothers and sisters to help me grow in my faith.

HOUSE RULES

*Finally, all of you, be like-minded, be sympathetic, love one another,
be compassionate and humble. Do not repay evil with evil or insult
with insult. On the contrary, repay evil with blessing, because
to this you were called so that you may inherit a blessing.*
1 PETER 3:8–9 NIV

. . . .

Every family has some house rules: treat each other with kindness and
respect, no phones at the dinner table, don't put each other down, Dad
gets the last scoop of ice cream, no screen time until all the chores are
done, and so on. Do you have rules at your house?

Peter was writing some important rules for the family of believers.
He wanted them to be united and loving toward one another. Also like
a good parent, Peter wanted the family of God to be blessed.

Verses 10–11 (NLT) go on to say, "If you want to enjoy life and see
many happy days, keep your tongue from speaking evil and your lips
from telling lies. Turn away from evil and do good. Search for peace,
and work to maintain it."

Sounds like wise advice!

*Lord, thanks for giving us helpful rules to
keep the family happy and blessed.*

YOUR SAFE PLACE

*God is our safe place and our strength. He is always our
help when we are in trouble. So we will not be afraid,
even if the earth is shaken and the mountains
fall into the center of the sea.*
PSALM 46:1–2 NLV

Trauma counselors will often counsel their clients to think of a safe space in their mind. This can be a happy memory, a vacation spot, a favorite place to go every day—anywhere that feels completely safe in your mind. Many Christian counselors have their clients invite Jesus into that space to help process difficult memories.

The Bible tells us that God is our safe place. As you grow up, your safe places may change as you move and grow. But your safe place in God will never change. You can always count on Him to be the same.

God wants to protect you, to comfort you, and to tell you how loved you are. Sometimes sitting in the quiet with God is the best way to pray. Ask Him to fill you with His love as you sit in His presence. Picture yourself close to Jesus and let Him love you.

*Lord, You are always my safe place.
Thanks for giving me strength.*

LET GOD LOVE YOU

And so we know and rely on the love God has for us. God is love. Whoever lives in love lives in God, and God in them.
1 John 4:16 niv

Do you find it hard to simply be still? Some people are born with the "fidget gene." They always have to be moving something, jiggling their legs, fidgeting with something in their hands. People like that actually tend to think better while they're moving.

But even if you find that you must fidget, you can still learn to be still before God. This is simply sitting in God's presence and opening your heart up to God as He fills you and reminds you of His love (it's okay if you need to wiggle your legs or tap your fingers while you try this!).

In Psalm 46:10 (niv), God said, "Be still, and know that I am God; I will be exalted among the nations, I will be exalted in the earth."

God wants you to know that you are deeply loved just because you're you. He made you. He loves you. Nothing you can do will ever change that. Think about that for a while before you do anything else today. Let God love you.

Wow, God! You really love me just for being me.
I don't have to earn Your love. Thank You!

81

HUMAN BEING OR HUMAN DOING?

This is love: not that we loved God, but that he loved us
and sent his Son as an atoning sacrifice for our sins.
1 John 4:10 niv

It's easy for Christians to get into the bad habit of feeling like we're not doing enough. That we have to be a better Christian so that God will love us and approve of us. That we have to get it right all the time or we must stink at following Jesus. That we have to say yes to everything at church and sign up for every good deed so that God and everyone around us will know that we are Christians.

But that's not the Jesus way. God wants to fill us up with His love first and foremost, and then He pours out that love to others as the Holy Spirit leads us day by day. God made you a human *being*—not a human *doing*. Be listening for His leading in your life before you say yes to anything. You have nothing to prove. You are chosen and dearly loved just for *being*.

Lord, I'm guilty of trying to earn love and acceptance from
You and others. I'm sorry for that. Please fill me up with Your
love and give me ears to hear Your leading in my life.

THE THREE A'S

But God demonstrates his own love for us in this:
While we were still sinners, Christ died for us.
Romans 5:8 niv

· ·

Speaking of trying to earn love and acceptance. . . Let's talk about the three A's: acceptance, approval, and affirmation.

Most humans tend to walk around hunting for these three A's. They want to be accepted. They want to be approved of. They want others to affirm them. Many will go to extreme lengths to have these needs met. But did you know that Jesus has already taken care of these? We're going to dive into these over the next few days. But first, take a look at this: "Christ arrives right on time to make this happen. He didn't, and doesn't, wait for us to get ready. He presented himself for this sacrificial death when we were far too weak and rebellious to do anything to get ourselves ready. . . . But God put his love on the line for us by offering his Son in sacrificial death while we were of no use whatever to him" (Romans 5:6, 8 msg).

Heavenly Father, open my heart and mind to understand
Your amazing love for me. While I was still a mess, while I
was still making bad choices—You loved me even then.

YOU ARE ACCEPTED

"All those the Father gives me will come to me,
and whoever comes to me I will never drive away."
JOHN 6:37 NIV

The Amplified Bible says it this way: "The one who comes to Me I will most certainly not cast out [I will never, never reject anyone who follows Me]."

This is one of those verses to write down in your journal or on a sticky note. You're going to need it throughout your life. Rejection stings. We all face it from time to time. Whether it's not getting an invitation you are hoping for, finding no seat at the table you want to sit at, watching the boy you like choose another, or receiving a rejection letter from your college of choice, rejection hurts.

But something to remember in the midst of that is that you are always accepted in Christ. "Rejected" is not who you are. When rejection comes, acknowledge the hurt. Take it to Jesus. Let Him love you through it. And then start rejecting any lies the enemy flings at you. Stand on the truth that you are accepted forever.

You are loved.

Chosen.

His.

Lord, You know I've felt rejected at different times.
I bring that to You now. Please heal up those places as
I reject any lies the enemy has labeled me with.

YOU ARE APPROVED OF

For the LORD delights in his people;
he crowns the humble with victory.
PSALM 149:4 NLT

. . . .

Yes, God approves of you. Now let's clarify that: we're not talking about the things you do but about who you are. Make sense?

We all mess up. We choose selfishness sometimes. We choose sin. And like a good parent, God doesn't always approve of your choices. But He always approves of who you are.

Would a good and loving parent approve of their usually delightful toddler's behavior when she hits her sibling over the head with something hard? No. That toddler is getting appropriate consequences for what she's done so she learns that it's wrong to hit and not to do it again. But those consequences also show how much that child is loved and valued. That child's parents still love that child unconditionally no matter what she's done. They still approve of who she is, just not her behavior at the moment.

God's Word tells you that He delights in you no matter what you do or don't do. You're His precious child, and He loves you for who you are.

Lord, I think I'm starting to get it: Your love has nothing to do with my behavior. That's amazing love!

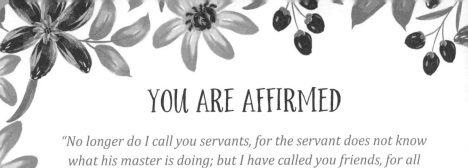

YOU ARE AFFIRMED

"No longer do I call you servants, for the servant does not know what his master is doing; but I have called you friends, for all that I have heard from my Father I have made known to you."
JOHN 15:15 ESV

So what is affirmation, anyway? Dictionary.com says *affirm* can mean "to support (someone) by giving approval, recognition, or encouragement." Who isn't going around looking for encouraging support? That's how we find our friends, right?

But Jesus took care of this for us too. Sometimes we lose our support system, like when we move or have a serious disagreement with a friend. If we were to lose our affirmation when we lose our friends, that would be devastating! But Jesus wants us to find our affirmation in Him first.

- He is our support: "They attacked me at a moment when I was in distress, but the LORD supported me" (Psalm 18:18 NLT).
- He gives us recognition: "The sheep hear his voice, and he calls his own sheep by name and leads them out" (John 10:3 ESV).
- He gives us encouragement: "You, LORD, hear the desire of the afflicted; you encourage them, and you listen to their cry" (Psalm 10:17 NIV).

Jesus calls us friend.

Jesus, thanks for calling me Your friend. I love You.

WHEN YOU'RE FEELING DOWN

The righteous cry out, and the LORD hears them;
he delivers them from all their troubles.
PSALM 34:17 NIV

- -

Anne of Green Gables used to talk about "Jonah days." When the bad things just keep piling up. Those days happen in this broken world, and when they do, these truths from God's Word can help:

- "The LORD is close to the brokenhearted and saves those who are crushed in spirit" (Psalm 34:18 NIV).
- "But God gives comfort to those whose hearts are heavy" (2 Corinthians 7:6 NLV).
- "Cast all your anxiety on him because he cares for you" (1 Peter 5:7 NIV).
- "Come to me, all you who are weary and burdened, and I will give you rest" (Matthew 11:28 NIV).
- "Trust in the LORD with all your heart and lean not on your own understanding; in all your ways submit to him, and he will make your paths straight" (Proverbs 3:5–6 NIV).

Chosen one, God sees you. He's close. Take these truths to heart as you let God love and comfort you.

Lord, I believe the truths I read in Your Word. I believe
You are close. Please comfort me. Please hide these
words in my heart as I bring my feelings to You.

THE LIFTER OF MY HEAD

You, LORD, are a shield around me, my glory,
the One who lifts my head high.

PSALM 3:3 NIV

Have you ever hung your head in shame before? You didn't want to talk to anyone because nobody could help. You just wanted to be left alone. God sees you, friend. The Bible says that He is the lifter of your head.

Imagine Jesus coming to you in your sadness, shame, and distress. You need not feel shame in His presence. Picture Him gently lifting your head and you looking straight into His eyes. What do you see there?

If it's not love and mercy and grace that you see there, then it's not from God. You can talk anything out with Jesus. He loves you and accepts you just as you are. He will show you what is wrong and what needs to be cleaned out of your heart. He will tell you the truth. He will show you love.

Remember this: you can boldly approach the throne of grace with confidence to find grace in your time of need (Hebrews 4:16).

Jesus, thank You for Your unfailing love for me no matter what I've done. Clean my heart. Fill it with Your grace and love. Change my heart to be like Yours.

HIS PRIZED POSSESSION

He chose to give birth to us by giving us his true word.
And we, out of all creation, became his prized possession.
JAMES 1:18 NLT

. . . .

Looking up Bible verses in several different translations and paraphrases can be fun, and it can help us get a better understanding of what verses mean. If you have a Bible app, looking up verses in multiple translations is easy.

Check out today's verse in a few different variations:

Amplified Bible: "It was of His own will that He gave us birth [as His children] by the word of truth, so that we would be a kind of first fruits of His creatures [a prime example of what He created to be set apart to Himself—sanctified, made holy for His divine purposes]."

The Message: "He brought us to life using the true Word, showing us off as the crown of all his creatures."

International Children's Bible: "God decided to give us life through the word of truth. He wanted us to be the most important of all the things he made."

What does all of this tell us? God gave us life through His true Word, and we are the crown of His creation. His most prized possession. Set apart and made holy for His divine purpose!

Wow, God! You see me as a valuable prize.
Thank You for giving me worth and value!

COUNT YOUR BLESSINGS

Let all that I am praise the Lord; may I
never forget the good things he does for me.
PSALM 103:2 NLT

Check out these lines from the old hymn "Count Your Blessings":

When you are discouraged, thinking all is lost. . .
Count your many blessings, name them one by one,
And it will surprise you what the Lord hath done.

Do you have a journal? If not, grab a blank notebook and start to record what you're thankful for every day. If you don't have a notebook, you could even find some blank space at the bottom of each of these devotions. The point is to get in the habit of thanking God for all the good things He's done for you.

You may be thinking, *How could I ever forget what God's done?* But when times are hard or you're in pain, it can be easy to focus on the problems instead of God's blessings. And if you have lots of blessings written down, you can go back to them and see the days when God was working. The days when He answered your prayers. The days when He blessed you.

Give it a try, and you might be surprised at all the Lord has done!

Lord, I'm so thankful for all You've done in my life.

JESUS PRAYS FOR YOU

*"I do not pray for these alone. . .but also for [all] those who
[will ever] believe and trust in Me through their message,
that they all may be one; just as You, Father, are in Me and
I in You, that they also may be one in Us, so that the world
may believe [without any doubt] that You sent Me."*
JOHN 17:20–21 AMP

Did you know that Jesus prayed for you? Not only is His prayer for you written out in John 17, but other scriptures tell us that Jesus is still praying for you now. We'll look at them in the coming days.

Check this one out next: Romans 8:34 (NLV) says, "Who then can say we are guilty? It was Christ Jesus Who died. He was raised from the dead. He is on the right side of God praying to Him for us."

Isn't it awesome how much Jesus cares for you? He prayed for you when He stood on the earth in human form, and He's in heaven praying for you now.

*Jesus, thank You for loving me so much! It brings my
heart joy to know that You are praying for me!*

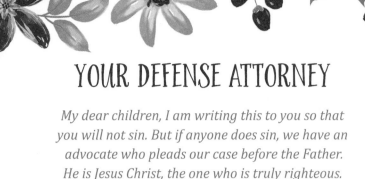

YOUR DEFENSE ATTORNEY

My dear children, I am writing this to you so that you will not sin. But if anyone does sin, we have an advocate who pleads our case before the Father. He is Jesus Christ, the one who is truly righteous.
1 JOHN 2:1 NLT

Bethany was a good kid. She loved Jesus. Loved being part of her church. Loved serving others. But when she turned sixteen, she was allowed some freedoms she'd never had before. She was allowed to be on social media, and she had her own job. As her life got busier, her downtime was spent online. Her relationship with Jesus took a back seat.

Pretty soon Bethany's online world was speaking louder than her faith. She kind of forgot who she was. Little by little, she started making poor choices and found herself in some real trouble. The kind where police officers and courts get involved. Although she hoped and prayed for a way out, she knew she deserved the consequences she might receive. These consequences definitely helped her turn to God again. She needed a good defense attorney in real life and in heaven. Find out more about Bethany's story tomorrow.

Lord Jesus, thank You for coming to my rescue time and time again. Help me to make my relationship with You top priority in my life.

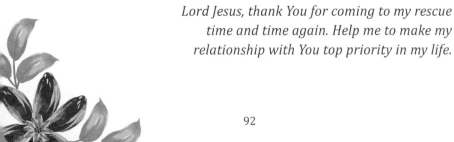

FREE FOREVER

Therefore He is able also to save forever (completely, perfectly, for eternity) those who come to God through Him, since He always lives to intercede and intervene on their behalf [with God].
HEBREWS 7:25 AMP

. . . .

Bethany's future is still unknown at this point. She is waiting for judgment in her situation. But in the spiritual realm, her future is secure. Jesus is the very best defense attorney. Jesus is "the way, the truth, and the life" (John 14:6 NLT). No one comes to the Father except through Him. Jesus stands before God and makes a way for Bethany, and for all of us, to be made right before God.

Bethany has repented of her sin. She gave her life back to Jesus and was relieved to be found out so she could be free again. She didn't want to continue being a slave to her sin. She doesn't know yet what might happen here on earth because of her poor decisions, but she knows that God sees her as clean and holy because of Jesus. She is free in Christ no matter what happens.

Jesus, You gave Your life to set me free forever.
I love You, Lord. Thank You!

WHEN YOU TURN BACK

"Simon, Simon, Satan has asked to sift all of you as wheat.
But I have prayed for you, Simon, that your faith may not fail.
And when you have turned back, strengthen your brothers."
LUKE 22:31–32 NIV

Before Jesus was betrayed by Judas and arrested, He was eating the Passover meal with His disciples. Jesus had something important to tell Simon here in Luke 22. Basically, Satan asked permission to smash the disciples. And troubles would come, for sure. But Jesus prepared and encouraged Simon Peter with these words. Jesus was praying for him, and He gave Peter direction for after he was tested.

A little later, Simon Peter denied Jesus three times because he was afraid. When Simon Peter realized what he had done, he wept. But God wasn't done with Simon Peter yet, even after he denied Jesus.

Jesus had instructed Peter to strengthen his brothers after he turned back. And that's exactly what Peter did. He was even a major part of establishing the early church.

God can use you even after you've messed up too. We all make mistakes. And when you turn back to Jesus, you can share your story with others to encourage them in their faith.

Lord, please use my mistakes to help others in their faith.

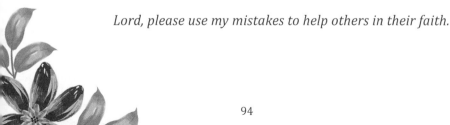

YOU BELONG

*Just as our bodies have many parts and each part has a
special function, so it is with Christ's body. We are many
parts of one body, and we all belong to each other.*
ROMANS 12:4–5 NLT

Jessa walked into youth group for the very first time. Thankfully, she saw a friend she knew from drama group, and she instantly felt better. But those first few minutes of looking around at a new group of people can be a bit intimidating, right?

Here's the good news: Jesus says you belong! Especially at church. He made you a special part of His body, a.k.a. the church. The Bible says that Christ's body is made up of many parts and each of them is important.

The next time you walk into a room not knowing anyone, remember that Jesus is with you. Ask Him for courage to go and talk with someone new. Ask Him to show you where you belong, and try not to worry about what others think of you. Jesus knew exactly what He was doing when He made you part of His body. And you belong there!

Lord, thank You for making me a special part of Your body.

YOU BELONG WITH JESUS

"And be sure of this: I am with you always,
even to the end of the age."
MATTHEW 28:20 NLT

Kiera had a difficult time in grade school. She was bullied by a person in authority at the school. She didn't tell anyone about it for months, but then finally her parents noticed that something was wrong. Kiera's personality was changing. They did some investigating and found out the truth. They took Kiera out of school and reported what happened to the school board. But some damage had already been done, so Kiera's parents took her to see a Christian counselor. That helped a lot.

Years later Kiera was triggered by something that reminded her of how she felt helpless in grade school. She told her mom about it, and they prayed together. As they were praying, Kiera invited Jesus into that memory that still troubled her from school long ago. As the bad memory played out in her mind, Jesus gave her a new vision. Kiera saw herself in the schoolroom, but this time Jesus came over to her and cupped her face in His hands. He told her, "No matter what happens and when you feel like you don't belong, you always belong with Me."

Jesus, thank You that You can turn my bad memories
into something good when I invite You into them!

THE OUTPOURING

*"It shall come about after this that I shall pour out
My Spirit on all mankind; and your sons and your
daughters will prophesy, your old men will dream
dreams, your young men will see visions."*
JOEL 2:28 AMP

· ·

We have a houseplant in our bathroom that doesn't need very much watering. But if we let it go too long, it gets really dry and droopy. Has your faith ever felt like that? It's amazing how as soon as we give the plant a drink, it pops right back up!

This verse in Joel is repeated in Acts 2:17. And Isaiah 44:3 (NIV) says, "I will pour out my Spirit on your offspring, and my blessing on your descendants." God wants to pour His Spirit all over you. If you're not feeling it, maybe it's time to spend some time with Jesus asking Him to do just that.

Get alone with God and ask Him to pour His Spirit out on you. Your faith needs a drink of living water.

*Lord, I ask for an outpouring of Your Spirit
in my life. I'm thirsty, Lord God, and You're
the only one who can fill me up!*

HEARING GOD'S VOICE

Whether you turn to the right or to the left, your ears will hear a voice behind you, saying, "This is the way; walk in it."
ISAIAH 30:21 NIV

. . . .

Many people think that God stopped speaking long ago. Don't believe it! Check out what the Bible says:

- "My sheep hear my voice, and I know them, and they follow me. I give them eternal life, and they will never perish, and no one will snatch them out of my hand" (John 10:27–28 ESV).
- "You shall walk after the LORD your God and fear him and keep his commandments and obey his voice, and you shall serve him and hold fast to him" (Deuteronomy 13:4 ESV).
- "Does he who supplies the Spirit to you and works miracles among you do so by works of the law, or by hearing with faith. . . ?" (Galatians 3:5 ESV).
- "As it is said, 'Today, if you hear his voice, do not harden your hearts as in the rebellion' " (Hebrews 3:15 ESV).

Lord Jesus, I want to hear Your voice in my life.
Show me what that looks like. Please open my ears,
my heart, and my mind to hear from You!

ALLOW GOD TO LOVE YOU

The LORD appeared to me (Israel) from ages past,
saying, "I have loved you with an everlasting love;
therefore with lovingkindness I have drawn you
and continued My faithfulness to you."
JEREMIAH 31:3 AMP

In church we are taught to share the gospel from a young age. And rightly so. But if you've been a Christian for a long time, you can forget that the gospel still applies to you too. "For God so loved the world" is meant for you. And sometimes you need a good reminder and a long refill of His love for you.

First John 4:19 (ESV) says, "We love because he first loved us." Today, take some time to crawl up into God's lap, lean your head on His shoulder, and let Him love you. Can you imagine that as you pray? Talk to Him about what's on your heart. But make sure to allow time to sit and be loved in His presence. Nothing else in life can fill you up the way God's love does. His love is kind, faithful, and everlasting.

I love You, Lord, because You loved me first. I'm so
thankful for Your everlasting and overwhelming love!

THE LIFE SHE ALWAYS WANTED

*Jesus answered her, "Everyone who drinks this water will be
thirsty again. But whoever drinks the water that I give him will
never be thirsty again. But the water that I give him will become
in him a spring of water [satisfying his thirst for God] welling
up [continually flowing, bubbling within him] to eternal life."*
JOHN 4:13–14 AMP

Trisha grew up in a Christian home. But that's all it was to her—her childhood home. The Christian faith never made it past her head into her heart. She spent years looking for life and love in other places: people, career, relationships that progressed to marriage, and even her vacation destinations as an adult. She kept searching for the good life and sometimes even for an escape from the one she'd built for herself.

Later in life she came to the realization that anytime she tried to find life outside of Jesus, she was sorely disappointed. Nothing filled her like she hoped it would.

She came across these verses as an adult and finally found the answer she'd been looking for her entire life. Jesus is the living water. Jesus is the life she'd always wanted.

*Jesus, thank You for being my living water.
Let me be satisfied in You alone.*

REAL LIFE

For you died [to this world], and your
[new, real] life is hidden with Christ in God.
COLOSSIANS 3:3 AMP

. . . .

When Trisha committed her life to Christ, everything changed. She died to this world and everything she thought would make her happy. Galatians 2:20 (NIV) helps explain this: "I have been crucified with Christ and I no longer live, but Christ lives in me. The life I now live in the body, I live by faith in the Son of God, who loved me and gave himself for me."

That's the victorious Christian life at work: aligning yourself with Jesus Christ and His plans and purposes for you every moment of every day. For Trisha, that meant allowing Jesus to work in her marriage, and she stopped trying to control everything. She even began praying about things like shopping and vacations. She wanted Jesus to be involved in all of those choices. She asked Jesus to start speaking to her during her job. He knows everything! He could definitely help her with any problem she faced. She began to live by faith that Jesus cared about everything she cared about.

I want You to be a part of my real, everyday life, Jesus.
Help me to be in conversation with You about everything.

HELD CLOSE TO HIS HEART

He tends his flock like a shepherd: He gathers the lambs in his arms and carries them close to his heart; he gently leads those that have young.
ISAIAH 40:11 NIV

The Bible talks a lot about God being our shepherd. Since most of us don't live on farms or have sheep these days, that might not mean much to you. But in Bible times, everyone knew about the life of a shepherd. A good shepherd protects the sheep from wild animals and cares for them when they get hurt or wander off. Shepherds make sure their sheep always have food and fresh water.

Jesus is our good shepherd. He carries us close to His heart. Check out what Jesus said about Himself in John 10:11 (NIV): "I am the good shepherd. The good shepherd lays down his life for the sheep." And in verse 14 (NIV) He says, "I am the good shepherd; I know my sheep and my sheep know me."

Can you picture yourself being held in the arms of Jesus as you pray? He wants to speak to you and for you to know Him personally. He wants you to know that you are loved.

Lord, be my good shepherd. Help me hear Your voice telling me how much You love me.

SECOND FIDDLE

Love each other with genuine affection,
and take delight in honoring each other.
Romans 12:10 nlt

* *

The Message explains it this way: "Love from the center of who you are; don't fake it. Run for dear life from evil; hold on for dear life to good. Be good friends who love deeply; practice playing second fiddle" (verses 9–10).

Playing second fiddle means you are okay with letting someone else take the lead. You don't need to be first or be the center of attention.

Hmm. How might you practice playing second fiddle? Try this: Imagine you're at youth group and the youth pastor says he has special ice cream treats for everyone! That's your favorite, so you run and jump in line. Why not imagine yourself going to the end of the line and letting others go first? Or better yet, offer to help pass out the treats to everyone else first? What other scenarios can you come up with?

When you are filled to overflowing with the love of God, it's so much easier to play second fiddle.

Jesus, forgive me for the times I try to get what I want first.
Help me to see others and put them first instead.

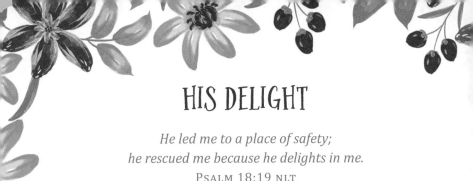

HIS DELIGHT

He led me to a place of safety;
he rescued me because he delights in me.
PSALM 18:19 NLT

Remember, before you took your first breath—before the creation of the world (Ephesians 1:4 tells us this!)—your worth was established. Your worth has nothing to do with your behavior. It has nothing to do with your choices. It has nothing to do with what you think or don't think. God loves you and delights in you simply because you are His creation. You're His precious child. He doesn't just tolerate you; He delights in you!

Think about how amazing that is! When God looks around at all of His creation, you are the best part! He chose you to be in relationship with Him. He leads you to places of safety. He rescues you from dangers—all because you are worth it to Him! He gave His very own life so that you could be with Him forever.

Doesn't that make you want to worship and praise God? Crank up your favorite worship song and sing your heart out in praise to the God who adores you!

Your love is amazing, God! You are so good
and kind. Thanks for loving me so deeply!

LIES FROM THE ENEMY

*"Then you will know the truth,
and the truth will set you free."*
JOHN 8:32 NIV

. . . .

After Jesus was baptized, He went to the desert and fasted for forty days and nights. Satan used that opportunity to try to tempt Jesus to sin. The Bible tells us that our enemy, Satan, is the father of lies. He will try every trick in the book to get you to mess up and believe those lies. So what did Jesus do when it happened to Him? He told Satan the truth from God's Word. And that's exactly what Jesus wants you to do too.

When you feel like you are being tempted to make a bad choice, ask Jesus for help. He's been there! He knows how to help you overcome. When Satan tries to trick you into believing a lie about yourself or God, find out what the truth is and use it against the enemy. When you memorize scripture, the Holy Spirit will help you remember those powerful words at just the right time.

*Lord God, I want to be strengthened by Your Word.
Help me to get into it, to learn it, to memorize it
and use it against the enemy when he attacks.*

LIES ABOUT YOURSELF

For the word of God is alive and powerful.
HEBREWS 4:12 NLT

. . . .

Yesterday we talked about the father of lies and what to do about him. Today we're going to talk strategy. The enemy really enjoys whispering lies to you about yourself. Take a look at some of these lies and how to counteract them:

Lie: You are ugly.

Truth: You are fearfully and wonderfully made (Psalm 139:14).

Lie: You are not smart enough.

Truth: God will give you wisdom (James 1:5).

Lie: This is too scary.

Truth: God hasn't given you a spirit of fear but of power, love, and a sound mind (2 Timothy 1:7).

Lie: You are alone.

Truth: God will never leave your nor forsake you (Hebrews 13:5).

Lie: You can't do anything right.

Truth: You can do anything God calls you to do through Christ who gives you strength (Philippians 4:13).

See how that works? Get in the habit of writing down any lies you are struggling with and finding the truth in God's Word. Remember: submit yourself to God, resist the enemy, and he will flee (James 4:7).

Jesus, thank You for showing me exactly what to do when the enemy tries to lie to me!

LIES ABOUT GOD AND FAITH

"Teach them your word, which is truth."
JOHN 17:17 NLT

After you've started counteracting Satan's lies with truth from God's Word, he'll start trying to get you to doubt that the Bible is even true at all. Don't fall for it.

Lie: God is mad at you.
Truth: There is no condemnation for those who are in Christ Jesus (Romans 8:1).

Lie: The Christian life is too hard.
Truth: Jesus will give you rest. His yoke is easy and His burden is light (Matthew 11:28–30).

Lie: God doesn't talk to people anymore.
Truth: Jesus said that His sheep hear His voice and follow Him (John 10:27).

Lie: The Bible isn't true.
Truth: God's Word is living and active and God-breathed (2 Timothy 3:16; Hebrews 4:12; 1 John 1:1).

Countless eyewitnesses saw all that happened with Jesus and His death and resurrection. From archaeologists finding locations in the Bible that were exactly as described to scientific evidence for the flood in Genesis, you can trust that God's Word is true and a reliable source to guide your life.

Thank You, Lord, that Your Word is truth!

NO ONE LIKE OUR GOD

Who has directed the Spirit of the Lord, or has taught Him as His counselor? With whom did He consult and who enlightened Him? Who taught Him the path of justice and taught Him knowledge and informed Him of the way of understanding?
Isaiah 40:13–14 AMP

When you're worried, when you're in trouble, when you're overwhelmed, when life seems too hard, remember this: your God is greater than any power on earth and in the heavens. And He knows you by name. He chose you as His own. He loves you dearly. You can go to Him with every problem and every need. He welcomes you in. He has a solution.

No legal system, no surgeon, no government, no authority in all the world can tell Him what to do! He is the ultimate authority over everyone and everything. As verse 9 (AMP) says, "Here is your God!" This is the God who rolls out the night sky every evening, knows all the stars by name, and is holding you (verse 26)!

There is no one like You, God! I'm so grateful that I can come to You with everything and know that You care.

A HOLY PURPOSE

"But you will receive power when the Holy Spirit comes upon you. And you will be my witnesses, telling people about me everywhere—in Jerusalem, throughout Judea, in Samaria, and to the ends of the earth."
ACTS 1:8 NLT

Is Jesus real or not? Can He help you? Does God still speak to His people today? The struggles, the blessings, the problems, and the adventures in your life all happen for a reason. God is using every single thing to tell you—and the world—that He is real. That He is close.

These lessons you're learning right now are not just for you. When you face something hard and have evidence that God is with you, write it down so you don't forget. Every time you hear from God, write it down in a journal. When God answers your prayers, make a note.

These life lessons have great purpose. They are to share with your friends, your parents, your future husband, your future children. God uses everything to bring hope, light, and love to a dark world.

Lord, I commit my life to You. Please use me for Your holy purposes in this world. I want to share the reality of who You are with the world!

COMING AND GOING

*The Lord will guard your going out and your coming in
[everything that you do] from this time forth and forever.*
PSALM 121:8 AMP

You are important to God. He sees you. The Bible says that He guards your coming and going—forever! That doesn't mean that you'll never get hurt or that bad things won't happen (life won't be perfect until heaven). It does mean that God has a plan and purpose for your life, and He will finish what He started in you. Philippians 1:6 (NLT) says, "And I am certain that God, who began the good work within you, will continue his work until it is finally finished on the day when Christ Jesus returns."

That means as you head out the door to church or school or camp, God sees you. As you make new friends and work your first job, God is with you. He is always available to talk with, get wisdom from, and remind you of your value and identity in Him. How can you reach out to God today during your coming and going?

*Lord, thank You for keeping constant watch over me.
Remind me throughout this day that You are close.*

LET GOD DIRECT YOUR STEPS

*The LORD directs the steps of the godly. He delights
in every detail of their lives. Though they stumble,
they will never fall, for the LORD holds them by the hand.*
PSALM 37:23–24 NLT

Katie turned sixteen and wanted a summer job. She went to two different job interviews. She had a bad feeling when she met the owner of one of the companies. The other company was a longer drive from her house, but she felt a peace about that job. She decided to go home and pray for God to show her which job to take.

God gives us gut feelings for a reason. Many times it's the Holy Spirit telling us something like an advanced warning signal. It's important to pay attention when you get feelings like that. Pray about it when it happens, and ask God to confirm what you think He is saying. Look in His Word for wisdom and truth.

When you seek God first, instead of asking Him to bless decisions you already made without Him, He will direct your steps.

*Lord, I want to follow You in every decision I make.
Help me to pay attention to Your warning
signals and to listen for Your direction.*

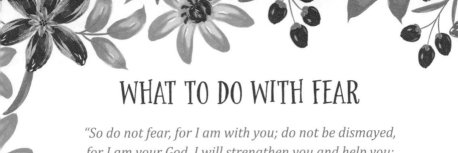

WHAT TO DO WITH FEAR

"So do not fear, for I am with you; do not be dismayed,
for I am your God. I will strengthen you and help you;
I will uphold you with my righteous right hand."
Isaiah 41:10 niv

The Bible has so much to say about fear! Let's check it out:

- "There is no fear in love, but perfect love casts out fear" (1 John 4:18 esv).
- "I sought the Lord, and he answered me; he delivered me from all my fears" (Psalm 34:4 niv).
- "This is my command—be strong and courageous! Do not be afraid or discouraged. For the Lord your God is with you wherever you go" (Joshua 1:9 nlt).
- "I am leaving you with a gift—peace of mind and heart. And the peace I give is a gift the world cannot give. So don't be troubled or afraid" (John 14:27 nlt).

We all find ourselves fearful from time to time. And God gives us the answer to that here: "When I am afraid, I put my trust in you" (Psalm 56:3 niv).

Lord, when I'm afraid, I bring all my thoughts
and fears to You. I know that You are near and
that You can help me through anything.

THE FEAR OF GOD

The LORD's delight is in those who fear him,
those who put their hope in his unfailing love.
PSALM 147:11 NLT

. . . .

Fearing God means that you honor and respect God with reverence and awe—not that you need to be afraid of a big, angry God in the sky. No, God delights in His children who are following Him and looking to Him for answers.

God is awesome and all-powerful. And He never fails. C. S. Lewis depicts Him as a lion in *The Lion, the Witch, and the Wardrobe*. Mr. Beaver tells Susan, who is nervous about meeting Aslan, "Safe? . . . 'Course he isn't safe. But he's good. He's the King, I tell you."[1]

The children and animals in this story have a healthy "fear" of Aslan's power and might. But they also understand that he is a good and loving king who wants the very best for his people.

Ask God to help you understand this concept. He is so good and loving, yet He deserves your utmost respect. His power is beyond all understanding. Psalm 145:3 (NIV) says, "Great is the LORD and most worthy of praise; his greatness no one can fathom."

Lord God, I believe You are all-powerful and all-knowing.
It's amazing to me that You care for me so deeply.

---

[1] *C. S. Lewis, *The Lion, the Witch, and the Wardrobe*
(New York: HarperTrophy, 1950), 86.

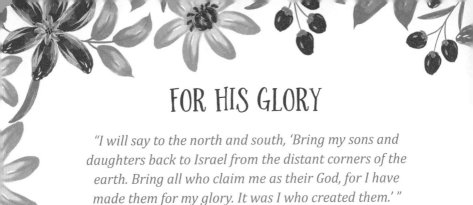

FOR HIS GLORY

"I will say to the north and south, 'Bring my sons and daughters back to Israel from the distant corners of the earth. Bring all who claim me as their God, for I have made them for my glory. It was I who created them.'"
ISAIAH 43:6–7 NLT

You've been chosen to be God's child. He made you for His glory. Second Corinthians 3:18 (NLT) says, "So all of us who have had that veil removed can see and reflect the glory of the Lord. And the Lord—who is the Spirit—makes us more and more like him as we are changed into his glorious image."

As you grow as a follower of Jesus, He changes your heart more and more to look like His. He's not taking away your personality. He made you that way on purpose. He is in the process of making you holy, more like Him in your thoughts and actions. You were made to know and love God and to reflect the glory of God to the world.

Lord, I invite You to keep changing my heart to look more and more like Yours. Help me think Your thoughts and walk in Your ways.

LIGHT FROM GOD'S WORD

Your word is a lamp to guide my
feet and a light for my path.
PSALM 119:105 NLT

Have you ever been in near-total darkness? The closest I can get to that around my house is in the basement. The main area doesn't have a single window. And when the doors are closed to the other rooms and the lights are out, you can't see a thing. Thankfully, we have lights going down the stairs to see until we get to the next light switch, which lights up the full basement.

God's Word is like that. It's a light to guide our feet and light up the path forward. When you don't know what to do next, head to God's Word. God loves to talk to you through His Word. He can light up darkness through His Word and help you get out of situations that aren't good. He can convict your heart through His Word and help you find the path to peace. He can lead you to your next step through His Word as you take time to seek Him.

Lord, please light up my path with Your Word.
Give me the desire to see what You have to say to me.

GOD WANTS YOUR HEART

*That is why the Lord says, "Turn to me now, while there
is time. Give me your hearts. Come with fasting, weeping,
and mourning. Don't tear your clothing in your grief,
but tear your hearts instead." Return to the Lord your God,
for he is merciful and compassionate, slow to get angry and
filled with unfailing love. He is eager to relent and not punish.*
JOEL 2:12–13 NLT

A friend was in a difficult situation. Her teenage daughter had made some really poor choices, and she was calling on other believers to help pray her daughter out of the mess she found herself in. Her daughter's heart had hardened toward God and His ways over the past few months. So we began to pray with our friend that her daughter would turn her heart back to Jesus.

Thankfully, that's exactly what happened. The daughter cried out to Jesus for help and repented of her sin. God is merciful and kind. He welcomed His daughter back into His arms.

As this scripture shows, God doesn't just want your good outward behavior; He wants your heart. And He's the only one who can see inside it.

Lord, You have my heart. Help me stay close to You.

116

LOOKING FOR MIRACLES

O Lord, You are my God; I will exalt You, I will praise and give thanks to Your name; for You have done miraculous things, plans formed long, long ago, [fulfilled] with perfect faithfulness.
ISAIAH 25:1 AMP

Have you experienced any miracles? Maybe you or someone you know was healed of an illness. Maybe you received an answer to something right in the nick of time. Maybe you saw something that doesn't make any physical sense.

God is in the miracle business. He always has been and always will be. He can do all the miracles you've heard of from long ago (the parting of the Red Sea, raising Jesus from the dead, healing multitudes), and He still does all kinds of miracles today. Just start looking around. Spend a few dollars at the store for a new notebook. Start writing down your prayer requests, and keep a record of all the answers and miraculous ways you start seeing God at work all around you. Some are little. Some are huge. God is still at work today—speaking, changing things, working on His kids' behalf.

I believe You are the God of miracles, Lord.
Help me to see You at work in my life.

HEALED AND SAVED

O Lord, if you heal me, I will be truly healed;
if you save me, I will be truly saved.
My praises are for you alone!
JEREMIAH 17:14 NLT

Jeremiah was a prophet in the Old Testament. His job was to share messages with God's people so that they would turn their hearts back to God. But God's people had forgotten Him. They were choosing sin and idols instead of following God's ways. In Jeremiah 2:13 (NLT), God said, "For my people have done two evil things: They have abandoned me—the fountain of living water. And they have dug for themselves cracked cisterns that can hold no water at all!"

But God offered a way out. If they would repent and turn back to Him, He would heal and save them. He offers us the same thing today. When God heals us, we are truly healed. When He saves, He saves completely.

Turning to people or things to heal and save us will never work. Only God can heal and save completely.

Lord, I choose You. You are the fountain of living water,
the only one able to heal and save the way I need.

A DAY OF WORSHIP

*Shout with joy to the L*ORD*, all the earth! Worship the
L*ORD *with gladness. Come before him, singing with joy.
Acknowledge that the L*ORD *is God! He made us, and we
are his. We are his people, the sheep of his pasture.*
PSALM 100:1–3 NLT

• •

Do you enjoy singing and listening to music? You don't have to be a
good singer to worship God. He loves to hear your praises no matter
what you sound like. Psalm 71:8 (NIV) says, "My mouth is filled with
your praise, declaring your splendor all day long."

So let's try that. Put a bunch of worship songs together in whatever way works best for you: song app, CDs, YouTube, on your piano
or guitar—whatever way you have available with the least amount
of outside distractions. Now spend your day worshipping Jesus. As
you clean your room and do homework, let the praise flow! As you
do chores around the house, thank Him in song. Whatever you have
going on that day, keep your focus on Jesus in praise and thanks. You'll
be amazed at how this changes your heart, your attitude, and the
atmosphere around you!

*Lord, I worship You with all my heart!
You are so amazing!*

ETERNAL CHOICES

"Today I have given you the choice between life and death, between blessings and curses. Now I call on heaven and earth to witness the choice you make. Oh, that you would choose life, so that you and your descendants might live!"

DEUTERONOMY 30:19 NLT

In the Old Testament, Moses was talking to the Hebrews and urging them to follow God and His ways. Their very lives and the lives of their children were at stake.

When someone makes a decision to follow Christ, it changes not only their lives but the lives of those around them and even their children's children. It has a trickle effect. That means that the goodness and blessing of living the Christian life gets passed on in families and relationships. Each individual person is still responsible to choose Christ or not, but the love and opportunity are there.

You get to make this same life-or-death decision. Choosing Christ means choosing life for eternity. Choosing sin now may mean death for eternity. The enemy is really good at making sin look good and easy now. But it has eternal consequences.

What will you choose?

Lord God, I choose life. I choose Your ways. I want to follow You and have life for all eternity. Let this blessing be passed on to my family as I share Your love with them.

HEALTHY CHOICES

A peaceful heart leads to a healthy body;
jealousy is like cancer in the bones.
PROVERBS 14:30 NLT

Ellie had a lot of anxiety. She worried about what others thought of her, and she'd often feel jealous if someone else received something that she didn't. She was hurt when she didn't get team captain on her sports team. She had a hard time feeling happy for her friend who did get that position.

Sadly, Ellie's anxiety started to affect her body. Her heart rate would speed up, and she even started getting heart palpitations. She went to see the doctor because she was scared something was really wrong with her.

But Ellie's problem turned out to be a heart problem at its root. Not her physical heart. Ellie's mom started praying with her and for her. Ellie began to talk to Jesus about her worries and fears. She repented of being jealous and worrying about everything. She began looking up scriptures about her identity and worth. This helped her to stop worrying about what other people thought. These healthy choices made all the difference in Ellie's life, and her body started feeling better too.

Jesus, I need Your help to keep my heart healthy—
physically and spiritually. Show me how to make
healthy choices with my body, mind, and spirit.

THE SERVANT'S APRON

*And all of you, dress yourselves in humility as
you relate to one another, for "God opposes
the proud but gives grace to the humble."*
1 PETER 5:5 NLT

Have you ever dressed yourself in humility? The Amplified Bible helps explain this scripture: "And all of you, clothe yourselves with humility toward one another [tie on the servant's apron], for God is opposed to the proud [the disdainful, the presumptuous, and He defeats them], but He gives grace to the humble."

Tying on the servant's apron can be difficult, right? Especially when you're hungry or tired. It's hard to let others go first at times. But God promises to take care of all your needs. Anything that God wants for you will happen. You can trust that He's watching out for you and taking care of you. So don't be afraid to tie on the servant's apron to help others and let others go first. You'll be blessed in the process.

*Lord, please forgive me for my selfishness at times.
Help me to learn to put others first and to serve
them. I trust You to take care of all my needs.*

HUMILITY

Who among you is wise and intelligent? Let him by his good conduct show his [good] deeds with the gentleness and humility of true wisdom.

JAMES 3:13 AMP

. . . .

A mother was talking to her young daughter who was being extra sassy at the moment. The mom patiently tried to tell her daughter about kindness, respect, and humility. She asked her daughter, "Do you know what humility is?" The young girl put her hands on her hips, rolled her eyes, and said, "Of course I do!"

While that seems funny, it's not far off from what many of us do as we grow older. We want to be humble, but inside we want our own way a little bit more.

Psalm 25:9 (NLT) says, "[The LORD] leads the humble in doing right, teaching them his way." If you're honest with yourself, you may struggle with humility a little more than you think. And when that happens, it's time to come to Jesus. Repent of selfishness and pride. Ask Jesus to teach you how to be humble. Let Him lead you.

Jesus, forgive me for my selfishness and pride. I'm sorry when I act like a know-it-all. Change my heart. Show me how to be genuinely humble.

123

I'M SORRY!

Come close to God, and God will come close to you.
Wash your hands, you sinners; purify your hearts,
for your loyalty is divided between God and the world.
JAMES 4:8 NLT

Nathan and his sister Olivia were in the middle of one of their daily arguments. Mom had to come and mediate again. Olivia needed to apologize this time. "I'm sorry, okay?" she said as she stomped off to her room. But she wasn't really sorry; she was just saying the words.

Sometimes we come to God like that—a quick sorry to get through the prayer and feel a little better about our sin. But check out what James 4:9–10 (NLT) says: "Let there be tears for what you have done. Let there be sorrow and deep grief. Let there be sadness instead of laughter, and gloom instead of joy. Humble yourselves before the Lord, and he will lift you up in honor."

That sounds a lot different than "I'm sorry, okay?" doesn't it? It's being truly repentant, not just sorry you got caught. The Amplified Bible says this in verse 10: "Humble yourselves [with an attitude of repentance and insignificance] in the presence of the Lord, and He will exalt you [He will lift you up, He will give you purpose]."

Lord, help me to truly humble myself before You
when I've done wrong. Please purify my heart.

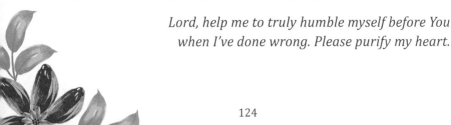

RESTORATION AND VICTORY

*But he was pierced for our rebellion, crushed for
our sins. He was beaten so we could be whole.
He was whipped so we could be healed.*
ISAIAH 53:5 NLT

- -

Why is it important to take our sin seriously? Because God did. He sent His Son to die for our sins. That's why saying, "I'm sorry, okay?" and stomping off just doesn't cut it. God wants our hearts. He wants full repentance, where we are truly sorry for the sin that caused Jesus to die. It's a big deal.

Once we've come to Jesus and confessed our sins in repentance, He doesn't want us to live in shame and defeat anymore. Psalm 34:5 (NIV) says, "Those who look to him are radiant; their faces are never covered with shame."

When you come to God wholeheartedly, He cleanses you from your sin and sets you on the right path again. Your relationship with God is restored and you can move forward in victory.

*Jesus, I don't ever want to take Your death for granted.
You died to save me from my sin. I'm sorry for turning
away from You and choosing my own way. Please restore
our relationship and set me on the right path again.*

WISE WORDS

Don't be impressed with your own wisdom. Instead, fear the LORD and turn away from evil. Then you will have healing for your body and strength for your bones.
PROVERBS 3:7–8 NLT

Proverbs is a book about wisdom, so if you're in need of wisdom, it's the place to go. Many interesting proverbs, like the one above, suggest that what's going on in your heart and mind can affect your physical body. Basically, instead of being a know-it-all, honor God and keep away from evil. Doing this can help keep your body healthy.

Remember what the verses right before verses 7–8 say? Here's a reminder: "Trust in the LORD with all your heart; do not depend on your own understanding. Seek his will in all you do, and he will show you which path to take" (Proverbs 3:5–6 NLT).

Chew on these wise words today. If you want to stay healthy in heart and mind, and stay on the right path in life, follow Jesus!

I need wisdom, Lord. I'm growing up, and things feel overwhelming at times. Help me to stay on the right path with You.

THE PURSUIT OF JESUS

*And he said to her, "Daughter, your faith has
made you well. Go in peace. Your suffering is over."*
MARK 5:34 NLT

• •

A woman who had a bleeding disorder for many years came to Jesus to be healed. She'd spent everything she had trying to get well, and she was desperate. She was labeled as "unclean" because of her illness. Jewish law would have prevented her from being in close contact with most people.

But she hid among the crowd anyway and tried just to touch the hem of Jesus' tunic. She thought that if she did only that, she would be healed. She was right! At the moment she touched Jesus' clothes, her bleeding stopped and she was healed.

Jesus said it was her faith that made her well. She believed that Jesus had the power to change everything. And He healed her immediately.

Are you willing to pursue Jesus like this woman did by going against the culture to get close to Jesus?

*Lord Jesus, help me to be brave like this woman
You healed. It's so difficult to go against the culture
these days. Help me to pursue You no matter what.*

GO TO GOD FIRST

O LORD my God, I cried to you for help,
and you restored my health.
PSALM 30:2 NLT

Melanie had some sort of weird illness. She went to the doctor and had all kinds of tests. Nothing came back conclusive. So she started researching every little ache and pain. She found one site that would have one expert opinion. But then another site would have an expert saying the exact opposite. It was all so confusing! She also found a bunch of home remedies, supplements, and health treatments to try. She spent thousands of dollars trying to feel better.

After Melanie had exhausted her mind and bank account on research and supplements, she decided to start praying. And what she found was that God really did want to help her. He wanted to lead her to the right practitioners and health treatments that would really work. Little by little, as Melanie prayed and listened for God's leading, she was able to get to the bottom of her illness and find healing.

God can do anything. He can speak to you. He can heal. It's important to remember to go to Him first before going down a path that excludes Him.

God, I want our relationship to be my highest priority.
Help me to go to You first about everything!

GUARDRAILS

Where there is no [wise, intelligent] guidance, the people
fall [and go off course like a ship without a helm], but in the
abundance of [wise and godly] counselors there is victory.
PROVERBS 11:14 AMP

Have you ever taken a road trip up a mountain? It can be a little frightening. Most places have guardrails to prevent serious accidents like going over the side of the mountain. But some more remote places don't have guardrails. You have to keep your eyes on the road at all times or you might be in big trouble. The guardrails help keep you safe.

God gives us guardrails in life too. He puts wise people in your path to help you when you look like you might be a little too close to the edge. He has given you the Holy Spirit to give you warning signals when you're straying off the path He has for you.

If you are in need of wise counsel, talk to God about this. Ask Him to send you some godly mentors who can help when you need wisdom and answers for life's great adventures.

Lord, thanks for putting guardrails in my life.
Help me listen to wise counsel when You send it.

BUMPERS AND BOWLING

Therefore, [continue to] accept and welcome
one another, just as Christ has accepted and
welcomed us to the glory of [our great] God.
ROMANS 15:7 AMP

Kassidy wanted to go bowling for her birthday. She wasn't that good at it, but it sounded like fun. She got there with her family and a few friends, excited to knock down some pins. Her dad gave her a few pointers as she picked up her ball. She released the ball and watched it roll down the lane right into the gutter. She tried again. This time she gave it a little more speed and then watched it roll down the lane—right into the gutter again. And again. Ugh. She was not having fun. But then she learned about the bumpers. If the managers turned on a certain switch, the bumpers would prevent the balls from going into the gutter! Now all of Kassidy's balls made it to the pins. Bumpers helped Kassidy have fun in the game and not have to be a perfect bowler.

God gives you bumpers and guardrails in life too. He knows you aren't perfect, and He accepts and welcomes you as you are. When you're about to hit the gutter, God puts people and circumstances in your life to help you stay on the right path.

Lord, thanks for guardrails and bumpers in my life!

WHEN YOU TRIP UP

The godly may trip seven times, but they will get up again.
But one disaster is enough to overthrow the wicked.
PROVERBS 24:16 NLT

• •

Have you ever played a video game not knowing what you were doing? The game ended quickly, and you got to start all over. You tripped or fell or died again and again until you got the hang of it. Or remember when you were learning to ride a bike? You probably crashed a time or two, but someone was there to help. And especially when you were just learning to walk as a toddler, you tripped a bunch! But your parents were there to help you get up again.

This verse in Proverbs sounds a bit like that. God's children may trip, but He is with them and will help them get up again. But people who have no hope get completely overwhelmed when disaster strikes. They've not chosen to follow Jesus, and there is no one to help.

You can always count on Jesus to be with you when you trip up.

Jesus, I'm so thankful that You help me
up even if I trip again and again. I know
Your hand is there to grab ahold of.

PERFECT PEACE

You will keep in perfect peace all who trust in you, all whose thoughts are fixed on you!
ISAIAH 26:3 NLT

- -

Abby's dad was having open-heart surgery. He wasn't even that old! But he'd been born with a heart defect, and he knew he'd have to have it fixed one day. Thankfully, Abby's family knew and loved Jesus. They trusted in Him for peace. They trusted in His will for their lives.

The day of the surgery arrived. Even though the week leading up to the surgery was a little bit scary at times, they knew God was with them. Peace settled over them during the surgery. Abby knew that her dad's life was in God's hands. God kept the family in peace during the surgery, and they refused to worry about complications.

Abby's dad came through the surgery with a few hiccups. He had to stay in the ICU for a while. But he was alive, and the family trusted God to take care of him. Six days later, Abby's dad was able to go home. Abby's family learned that fixing their thoughts on Jesus and not their worries kept them in peace during that difficult time.

Jesus, thank You for giving us Your supernatural peace during hard times.

BIG PRAYERS AND YESES FROM GOD

For all of God's promises have been fulfilled in Christ
with a resounding "Yes!" And through Christ, our "Amen"
(which means "Yes") ascends to God for his glory.
2 CORINTHIANS 1:20 NLT

. . . .

My daughter Jessa broke her leg badly and had quite a few complications from that. Two other family members had some serious health issues going on at the same time. It felt overwhelming. We came together as a family and decided to pray big prayers. We had a long list. We asked God for answers and healing. We prayed for His intervention when we were confused by some things that the doctors were telling us. We did this over and over until the next appointment and decision came.

In my journal not long after, I was able to write these words: "So much blessing! God answered yes to every single prayer."

If you're facing something big, get your believing family together and pray big prayers. God hears you, and He will answer according to His will. James 5:16 (NLT) says, "Confess your sins to each other and pray for each other so that you may be healed. The earnest prayer of a righteous person has great power and produces wonderful results."

Thank You for hearing my prayers, God!

HOW TO WALK OUT YOUR FAITH

*This letter is from Peter, an apostle of Jesus Christ. I am
writing to God's chosen people who are living as foreigners.*
1 PETER 1:1 NLT

- -

For the rest of our time together, we're going to walk through the books
of 1 and 2 Peter and 1 John together. Why? Because they were written
to God's chosen people. And you're one of God's chosen people too!
These letters, written by Peter and John, were written to encourage
Christians in their faith so they would know how to follow Jesus in a
mixed-up world.

Walking out your faith with Jesus is a lifelong pursuit. As you get
to know about Him, learn to hear His voice in your life, and seek to
obey His will and His ways, you are walking out your faith. You don't
have to know it all at once. You don't have to worry about getting it all
right. Jesus is walking along with you, showing you the way. His Spirit
is alive in you, whispering truth and love (see Romans 5:5) to you at
all times (see John 14:16).

*God, thank You for Your Word that helps me know how
to walk out my faith. Thank You for Your Holy Spirit,
who makes Your Word come alive in my life.*

WALKING CLOSELY WITH GOD

God the Father knew you and chose you long ago,
and his Spirit has made you holy. . . . May God
give you more and more grace and peace.
1 PETER 1:2 NLT

. . . .

See? Here's another great reminder that God knew you and chose you long ago! Peter is praying that God would give His children more grace and peace. The Amplified Bible says, "May grace and peace [that special sense of spiritual well-being] be yours in increasing abundance [as you walk closely with God]."

Have you ever felt closer to God at certain times than at others? Like maybe at church or when you're singing worship music? But what is the truth? The truth is that no matter what it feels like, Jesus has promised never to leave you (Hebrews 13:5; Matthew 28:20). Get in the habit of picturing yourself walking closely with Jesus, arm in arm or hand in hand.

Hebrews 11:1 (NIV) says, "Now faith is confidence in what we hope for and assurance about what we do not see." When feelings get in the way of the facts, remind yourself of the truth. You can walk closely with God, and He is always with you!

Lord God, remind me of the truth that You
are close and that You'll never leave me.

THE FUTURE STARTS NOW

All praise to God, the Father of our Lord Jesus Christ. It is by his great mercy that we have been born again, because God raised Jesus Christ from the dead. Now we live with great expectation, and we have a priceless inheritance—an inheritance that is kept in heaven for you, pure and undefiled, beyond the reach of change and decay.
1 PETER 1:3–4 NLT

The Message paraphrase of these verses says, "Because Jesus was raised from the dead, we've been given a brand-new life and have everything to live for, including a future in heaven—and the future starts now!"

Heaven is real and waiting and glorious! Your inheritance is waiting there for you. God's Word promises that His chosen ones (you!) will live eternally with Him in heaven where " 'he will wipe every tear from their eyes. There will be no more death' or mourning or crying or pain, for the old order of things has passed away" (Revelation 21:4 NIV).

But you don't have to wait for heaven to start living a victorious and joyful life. The future starts now! As you walk closely with Jesus, He shows you the path of life and fills you with joy in His presence (Psalm 16:11).

> *God, I'm so thankful that You're with me,*
> *filling me with joy now and forever.*

136

PROMISES AND THANKS

*You are being kept by the power of God because you
put your trust in Him and you will be saved from
the punishment of sin at the end of the world.*
1 Peter 1:5 nlv

• •

Wow! What a promise! When you decided to follow Jesus, you became God's child. And the Bible says, "He cares about you [with deepest affection, and watches over you very carefully]" (1 Peter 5:7 amp).

Think about that for a minute. How does it make you feel that God cares about you deeply and watches over you very carefully? That you are being kept and held by the power of God? Consider writing these thoughts down in your journal.

Spend some time in prayer now, thanking God for being with you and watching over you. Praise Him for His deep love for you. Honor Him in your heart and mind. Thank Him for saving you from the punishment of sin and preparing a place for you in heaven. Tell Him how you feel about all of that.

God calls you chosen! Lift your heart to Him in worship.

*Lord God, I'm grateful to be called Yours!
I worship and honor You today.*

WORTH MORE THAN GOLD

*With this hope you can be happy even if you need to
have sorrow and all kinds of tests for awhile. These tests
have come to prove your faith and to show that it is good.
Gold, which can be destroyed, is tested by fire. Your faith is
worth much more than gold and it must be tested also.*
1 Peter 1:6–7 nlv

Would you want to ride in a car with a driver who went to driver's ed but never took the test? What about something bigger than that? Like an airplane! Would you want to be flying on a plane where the pilot never took a test to get a pilot's license? Probably not. What about you? How do you feel after taking a test? Probably glad that it's over but happy when you get a good grade, right? Now you and your teacher and others know how much you actually know about the subject.

When trials come at us, our faith gets tested. You can be thankful that when hard things come your way, God is always with you. He helps you through it. And when the test or trial is over, you've learned that God really was there with you. And your faith is real. And that's worth more than gold!

*Thanks, Lord, for strengthening my faith
and being with me in everything!*

BE LIKE THE HOLY ONE

Get your minds ready for good use. Keep awake. Set your hope now and forever on the loving-favor to be given you when Jesus Christ comes again. Be like children who obey. Do not desire to sin like you used to when you did not know any better. Be holy in every part of your life. Be like the Holy One Who chose you.
1 PETER 1:13–15 NLV

. . . .

These are some really important scriptures as a child of God. Jesus is coming soon! Are you ready? It's easy to get distracted with growing up and friends and school and endless activity. But remember that God has a special plan for your life. Set your mind and your hope on Jesus as you go through life. God calls you to obey. He wants you to be holy in all you do.

Whoa! That sounds hard. How is it possible to be holy in every part of your life? Remember that the Holy Spirit lives inside you, guiding you, teaching you, counseling you, and prompting you to follow Jesus in everything. He'll help you make decisions that honor God. He'll give you wisdom when you ask.

*Lord, I want to be like You. Fill me with
Your Spirit and help me to listen and obey.*

A GOOD FATHER

You call out to God for help and he helps—he's a good Father that way. But don't forget, he's also a responsible Father, and won't let you get by with sloppy living. Your life is a journey you must travel with a deep consciousness of God. It cost God plenty to get you out of that dead-end, empty-headed life you grew up in. He paid with Christ's sacred blood, you know.

1 Peter 1:17–19 msg

God is a good dad. He's not only good; He's perfect. He will never sin against you. He always gets it right. He sees the beginning of your life, all the way to the end. He sees what you can't. That's why trusting Him is so important. You can obey Him wholeheartedly. He wants the very best for your life.

Would a good dad let you go on hurting yourself through sin and bad choices? No, parents have a responsibility to correct and discipline their children. God, the perfect parent, disciplines those He loves too (Hebrews 12:6).

The good news is that God doesn't guilt and shame you. He wants you to repent by coming to Him and allowing Him to change your heart.

Lord, show me anything in my life that doesn't honor You. I want You to have my whole heart. Thanks for being the very best dad!

GROWING UP

So get rid of all evil behavior. Be done with all deceit, hypocrisy, jealousy, and all unkind speech. Like newborn babies, you must crave pure spiritual milk so that you will grow into a full experience of salvation. Cry out for this nourishment, now that you have had a taste of the Lord's kindness.
1 PETER 2:1–3 NLT

Peter has some direct commands to share. Stop every form of evil. Don't lie or be jealous. Say nice things! Pretty clear, right? These apply to Christians today too. You may think this should be easy for Christians, right? But many people struggle with jealousy, and it can be hard to say nice things to a crabby teenage brother sometimes!

Like newborn babies who need their mamas, you need the Holy Spirit to help you grow as a child of God. You're never alone as you try to do the right thing. God is good and kind, and He helps you carry out His will through His Spirit alive and at work in you!

God, thank You for Your kindness to me.
Thanks for giving me Your Spirit to help me
know right from wrong and to grow up in You!

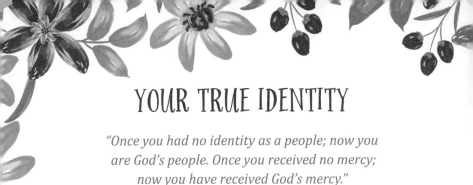

YOUR TRUE IDENTITY

"Once you had no identity as a people; now you
are God's people. Once you received no mercy;
now you have received God's mercy."
1 PETER 2:10 NLT

. . . .

This verse comes right after an awesome verse that we've talked about before, but it's always good to be reminded that "you are a chosen people, a royal priesthood, a holy nation, God's special possession, that you may declare the praises of him who called you out of darkness into his wonderful light" (1 Peter 2:9 NIV).

That's where your identity comes from. Not in what you do or your looks or special talents. Your identity comes from God because you're His kid. He chose you. He calls you royalty. You are His. He called you out of the dark and into the light.

Whenever you're tempted to worry that you aren't enough, remember these verses. Write them down. Ask the Holy Spirit to help you memorize them. He can bring them to your mind whenever you need them. Your identity is secure in Christ Jesus.

Lord, sometimes I feel like I'm not enough. Please remind
me of the truth that my identity is secure in You alone.

USING YOUR FREEDOM WISELY

Live as free people, but do not use your freedom as a cover or
pretext for evil, but [use it and live] as bond-servants of God.
1 PETER 2:16 AMP

. . . .

Jesus came to set us free. Freedom in Christ doesn't mean that we don't have to be responsible for our actions. Just the opposite. We have more responsibility because we represent Christ to the world. Freedom in Christ means that our salvation was a free gift from God, and it's nothing we could ever earn. It doesn't mean we are free to do whatever we want whenever we want.

Consider this: A good friend has diabetes and can't eat much sugar. You invite her over, and without thinking, you get out cookies and candy. You have all the freedom in the world to eat whatever you want. But it could hurt your friend, right? She might not have the willpower to say no.

This can apply to many situations. Try putting yourself in other people's shoes to help get understanding when faced with this kind of thing. Think about how you would like to be treated and don't abuse your freedom.

Lord, help me to use my freedom responsibly
and with a heart of love toward others.

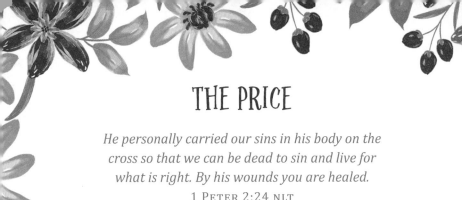

THE PRICE

He personally carried our sins in his body on the cross so that we can be dead to sin and live for what is right. By his wounds you are healed.
1 PETER 2:24 NLT

* *

The Message paraphrases this verse like this: "He used his servant body to carry our sins to the Cross so we could be rid of sin, free to live the right way. His wounds became your healing."

The price of taking away our sin, giving us freedom, and making a way for us to live forever in heaven with God was the death of His Son. First Peter 2:24 reminds us of this truth. Jesus died on the cross so that we can be free from sin—not a slave to it anymore. Completely dead to it. And now we are free to live the right way: trusting in Christ, listening for His voice in our everyday life, following His lead.

The next part of the verse is a stark reminder: "By his wounds you are healed."

As you take time to pray today, remember: your freedom from sin came at the highest price. Allow this to bring you to your knees in worship and thanksgiving. God loves you so much that He sent His Son.

Jesus, You sacrificed everything for me.
Help me live my life for You in return.

BEAUTY WITHIN

Don't be concerned about the outward beauty of fancy hairstyles,
expensive jewelry, or beautiful clothes. You should clothe yourselves
instead with the beauty that comes from within, the unfading
beauty of a gentle and quiet spirit, which is so precious to God.
1 PETER 3:3–4 NLT

Peter talked about beauty at the beginning of 1 Peter 3. In that time period, wealthy women would spend hours having their hair braided intricately and being dressed by their servants. Peter said that beauty comes from the inside, and that is a message we all need to be reminded of.

God gave you your body purposefully. You devalue God's creation when you turn from your mirror in disgust. Get in the habit of thanking God for every part of your amazing body. Even the parts you don't like. As you look in the mirror, begin thanking God for every part of you. That your eyes can see. That your ears can hear. That your teeth can chew to keep you healthy. Instead of feeling defeated by the flaws you see, ask God to help you take good care of the body He gave you, and trust in faith that He will.

Creator God, help me to see myself as You
see me: beautiful from the inside out.

BETTER THAN VITAMINS

For the Scriptures say, "If you want to enjoy life and see many happy days, keep your tongue from speaking evil and your lips from telling lies. Turn away from evil and do good. Search for peace, and work to maintain it. The eyes of the LORD watch over those who do right, and his ears are open to their prayers. But the LORD turns his face against those who do evil."
1 PETER 3:10–12 NLT

This little nugget of truth for life is tucked away in the book of 1 Peter, and it's better than your daily vitamin. Want to see happy days? Follow God's plan for your life! Verse 11 in the Amplified Bible explains it this way: "He must turn away from wickedness and do what is right. He must search for peace [with God, with self, with others] and pursue it eagerly [actively—not merely desiring it]."

God is watching over you, and His ears hear your prayers. He is with you, helping you to follow Him throughout your life. His Spirit prompts you to turn away from evil and to pursue God. This doesn't mean that life won't be hard sometimes. But it does mean that God will help you enjoy the life He gave you!

My happiness is found in You, Lord.
Help me follow Your ways.

GET READY!

But in your hearts revere Christ as Lord. Always be prepared to give an answer to everyone who asks you to give the reason for the hope that you have. But do this with gentleness and respect, keeping a clear conscience, so that those who speak maliciously against your good behavior in Christ may be ashamed of their slander.

1 PETER 3:15–16 NIV

. . . .

If you love God and treat other people with kindness, people are going to wonder what makes you different. They may even ask you questions about why you act the way you do. Get ready to share!

Some people will disagree with your faith in unkind ways. But before you get angry, ask for God's help. He is right there with you, and He sees everything that's happening. He wants you to answer with gentleness and respect, not anger and embarrassment.

The reason people ask is because they are looking for hope too! And they want to know if yours is real or not!

God, help me remember that everyone else is looking for hope in You too. You created them that way. Help me be gentle and respect others when I share my faith in You.

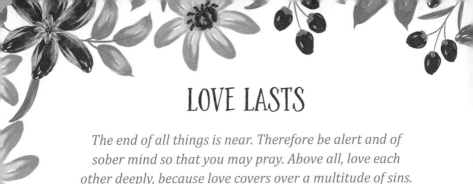

LOVE LASTS

The end of all things is near. Therefore be alert and of sober mind so that you may pray. Above all, love each other deeply, because love covers over a multitude of sins.
1 PETER 4:7–8 NIV

"The end of all things is near." This sounds like a quote from the *Lord of the Rings* movies! But Jesus really is coming back. The Bible promises this is so. Epic movie series like *Lord of the Rings* and *The Chronicles of Narnia* point to the restoration of our world and the return of our King.

So keep on praying and following Jesus along the way. Keep your focus on Jesus, and He will lead you in love. School, hobbies, careers, and things are given to you for the time being and can be used to share God's love—but love is the most important thing. We need to share the love of God with others while we await Jesus' return.

When you love others deeply and put their needs above your own, you are representing Christ to a world that desperately needs to be loved.

Lord, help me to keep my focus on You and not get too distracted by earthly things that pass away. Help me love others deeply. That's what lasts.

SHOWING LOVE THROUGH YOUR TALENTS

Each of you should use whatever gift you have received to serve others, as faithful stewards of God's grace in its various forms. If anyone speaks, they should do so as one who speaks the very words of God. If anyone serves, they should do so with the strength God provides, so that in all things God may be praised through Jesus Christ. To him be the glory and the power for ever and ever. Amen.
1 PETER 4:10–11 NIV

Everyone has talent of some sort. You may not be amazing at the piano, but you might be good at math. You might not be the next Picasso, but maybe God has gifted you at sports.

It's good to work at getting better at the talents God has given you. God wants to use your talents so that He can show His love to others through your special gifts.

How can you use your gifts and talents to help others? Can you help someone who is struggling in an area that you're really good at? Ask God to show you some special ways that you can use your gifts to help others and show God's love.

God, please show me ways that I can use my gifts to help others and spread Your love.

JOY IN TRIALS

Dear friends, don't be surprised at the fiery trials you are going through, as if something strange were happening to you. Instead, be very glad—for these trials make you partners with Christ in his suffering, so that you will have the wonderful joy of seeing his glory when it is revealed to all the world.
1 PETER 4:12–13 NLT

When Julie became a Christian, she thought life was going to be easy. She was discouraged when a bunch of problems started coming her way. She thought the Christian life was supposed to be better than this.

But what she didn't know is that God was training her. He wanted to show her how to search for Him during difficult times. How to seek His will in all things so that she could have victory in her everyday life. He wanted to show her what real joy is, not just superficial happiness from pleasant circumstances. When things are going smoothly, that's not true peace. True peace is knowing that God is with you, leading you, guiding you, and speaking to you during hard times.

Jesus, I'm thankful I can find You in each hard thing.
I trust You will give me joy in Your presence!

ABILITIES AND PRIDE

So humble yourselves under the mighty power of God,
and at the right time he will lift you up in honor.
1 PETER 5:6 NLT

Are you awesome at basketball and other sports? Do you have a beautiful singing voice? Or maybe gymnastics is your thing. Whatever gifts and talents you have, it's okay to be confident in your skills and giftedness. God has given you those gifts for a purpose.

But God doesn't want you to be prideful about those gifts and abilities. Romans 12:3 (NLT) says, "Don't think you are better than you really are. Be honest in your evaluation of yourselves, measuring yourselves by the faith God has given us."

Your gifts can be used for God, to bring Him attention and glory, or they can be used to bring attention and glory to yourself. Which one will you choose? Here's the thing: People who brag about their talents usually don't have a lot of real friends. People who bring attention to Jesus have an inner joy that comes from loving Him. The choice is yours to make.

Lord, I'm thankful for the talents You've given me. I commit them to You. Let them bring You attention and glory.

GOD CARES

*Cast all your anxiety on him
because he cares for you.*
1 PETER 5:7 NIV

Sarah carried a lot of weight on her shoulders. She was a straight A student. She was on the varsity volleyball team. She had a science fair project coming up and a ten-page paper due. She had responsibilities at home and responsibilities at church. One day she came home from school and realized that she had said yes to too many things. She was struggling.

She felt guilty because she chose all of this herself and should've known better. So she shut God out. But God wants us to come to Him whether things are our fault or not. Even if we feel we deserve all the stress we're carrying. God wants to help carry it for you because He cares.

This is one of those verses to write down and tape on your mirror. Ask the Holy Spirit to help you memorize it because you'll need it a lot in this life.

God does care. He wants to help carry your burdens. Let Him.

*God, I bring my anxiety to You. I'm sorry I've
shut You out at times. Please help me.*

TRICKS OF THE ENEMY

Stay alert! Watch out for your great enemy, the devil.
He prowls around like a roaring lion, looking for someone
to devour. Stand firm against him, and be strong in your
faith. Remember that your family of believers all over the
world is going through the same kind of suffering you are.
1 PETER 5:8–9 NLT

. . . .

Even though the enemy knows he has already ultimately been defeated by Jesus, he's still trying his best to get into your head and discourage you so you won't be able to live well for God. That's why Jesus wants you to stay alert. Don't fall for Satan's tricks; he's the father of lies (John 8:44).

Remember that James 4:7 (AMP) says, "So submit to [the authority of] God. Resist the devil [stand firm against him] and he will flee from you." You have power in the name of Jesus to get rid of any evil you come up against.

You don't have to be afraid, just alert. Don't focus on fear of the enemy. Focus on Jesus and His power to fight your battles!

Lord, You have given me everything I need
to live my life for You. Help me to stay alert
and not fall for any of the enemy's tricks.

EVERYTHING WE NEED

His divine power has given us everything we need
for a godly life through our knowledge of him who
called us by his own glory and goodness.
2 Peter 1:3 niv

Barbara was a sweet elderly woman I met at church. She loved God with her whole heart and lived to serve Him. She became very dear to our family and taught us a lot about God. She carried on a conversation with Jesus constantly. She knew God's voice and shared with others how to hear Him too.

We didn't know it at the time, but her last mission on earth was to share this verse of scripture with our family. We had been going through a desperately hard time, and Barbara had been praying for us daily. She brought this verse to our home along with a gift. She said that God told her to share it with us.

The very next day Barbara fell and went to the hospital. She passed away the following week. This verse has been a constant in our family since then. We don't fight our battles in our own strength anymore. God's divine power gives us everything we need.

God, You are with me. I know I can face anything
the world throws at me because of Your divine
power alive and at work in me!

THE LIST

*For this very reason, make every effort to add to
your faith goodness; and to goodness, knowledge;
and to knowledge, self-control; and to self-control,
perseverance; and to perseverance, godliness; and to
godliness, mutual affection; and to mutual affection, love.*
2 PETER 1:5–7 NIV

Imagine if you were given a list like this and asked to get it done. Faith, goodness, knowledge, self-control. . .and on and on. Who could get all that right? You might be tempted to give up before you ever started!

Thankfully, the answer is given two verses earlier, before all of those questions are asked. Remember yesterday's important verse? Here it is again: "His divine power has given us everything we need for a godly life through our knowledge of him who called us by his own glory and goodness" (2 Peter 1:3 NIV).

This grocery list of godly values is long, but you don't have to work on them in your own power. It's God's "divine power" alive and at work inside of you that makes them happen. You are never alone!

*Lord God, this list is a bit intimidating. I'm trusting in
Your power at work inside me to help me fulfill it.*

NOT JUST A STORY

*For we were not making up clever stories when we told
you about the powerful coming of our Lord Jesus Christ.
We saw his majestic splendor with our own eyes.*
2 PETER 1:16 NLT

Peter was a part of Jesus' inner circle while He walked the earth. He saw Jesus heal and change people's lives. He witnessed miracles. He was there when Jesus' "appearance changed dramatically in their presence; and His face shone [with heavenly glory, clear and bright] like the sun, and His clothing became as white as light. And behold, Moses and Elijah appeared to them, talking with Jesus" (Matthew 17:2–3 AMP).

Peter was the one who wrote the book we're currently discussing in these devotions. He knew what he was talking about. He spent time with Jesus and knew Him well. Remember that as you read through the rest of 2 Peter. The Bible isn't just a book of old stories that can help you. They are the very words that God inspired people to write through the power of the Holy Spirit. Let the words take root in your heart and change you.

*Lord, thank You for Your Word and
the people You used to write it.*

FALSE TEACHERS

But there were also false prophets among the people, just as there will be false teachers among you. They will secretly introduce destructive heresies, even denying the sovereign Lord who bought them. . . . Many will follow their depraved conduct.
2 PETER 2:1–2 NIV

Grace grew up in church. She considered herself a strong believer and was part of a Bible study during high school. She went off to college and wanted to get into a group of believers there too. She made friends with a few girls who invited her to their Bible study. She was excited to go.

When she arrived, the girls were reading a book by an author she hadn't heard of. No Bible in sight. The author used scripture but had some strange ideas that didn't sit right with Grace. But her friends thought it was great, so she stayed. Weeks went by, and little by little Grace started agreeing with the weird ideas her friends believed. She had stopped reading her Bible altogether and was buying more books from the same author. By the end of the year, Grace decided the values she grew up with were ultraconservative, and she made some serious and life-changing decisions.

More about Grace tomorrow. . .

Lord, help me not to stray from Your
Word even if everyone else is doing it!

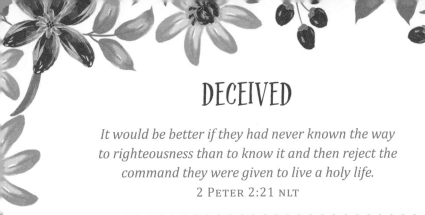

DECEIVED

*It would be better if they had never known the way
to righteousness than to know it and then reject the
command they were given to live a holy life.*
2 PETER 2:21 NLT

Grace started making big changes in her life. She started to explore things that she thought were off-limits to her. The author she was reading used scripture to back her ideas that she could do whatever made her happy. That sounded good to Grace's new college friends, and so Grace decided it sounded good to her too.

When she went home from college on her summer break, she went to a get-together with her old friends from youth group. They didn't recognize her anymore. One of Grace's good friends asked if they could go get coffee. She cared about Grace's life and prayed for her. She wanted to help.

But Grace enjoyed the way she was now. She wasn't interested in going back to "old-fashioned" ideas of faith. Grace's heart had become hard toward her former Christian friends and her family too.

*Lord, I know some people like Grace. Please give me
courage to reach out and pray for them! They've been
deceived. They fell for Satan's tricks. Please show me
how to love them and point them to Your truth.*

ANYTIME NOW

The Lord isn't really being slow about his promise, as some people think. No, he is being patient for your sake. He does not want anyone to be destroyed, but wants everyone to repent.
2 PETER 3:9 NLT

The Bible tells us that Jesus is coming back for all of us who love Him so that we can be with Him forever. James 5:7–8 (MSG) says, "Meanwhile, friends, wait patiently for the Master's Arrival. . . . Stay steady and strong. The Master could arrive at any time."

Many people wonder why Jesus hasn't come back already and removed all the bad things from this world. The Bible has an answer for that: God loves us, and He wants everyone to trust Him. So He is patient, giving people more time than they deserve to make a choice for Christ. His timing is perfect, and He knows exactly what He's doing. He wants people like Grace to repent and turn back to Him.

While we wait for Jesus' return, God wants us to be steady and strong in our faith.

God, please help me to be steady and strong as I wait for Jesus' return. Help me to share Your love with friends and family who need to know about You.

159

BECAUSE OF JESUS

*So then, dear friends, since you are looking forward
to this, make every effort to be found spotless,
blameless and at peace with him.*

2 PETER 3:14 NIV

Being spotless and blameless sounds like an impossible task, doesn't it? That's because it is. There is absolutely no way you can keep yourself spotless and blameless in your own strength. If you could, you wouldn't need Jesus, right? It's in Christ's strength alone that we are made holy.

When God looks at you, He sees you as spotless and blameless because Jesus took all of your sin and made you perfectly clean. That's how you have peace with God. The only way you can live a spotless and blameless life in this confusing world is in the power of Jesus Christ Himself. He's the one at work in you. When you get close to Him, He'll help you sort out the good from the sneaky and evil. Aligning yourself with Him and His Word daily is how you keep from being deceived by the enemy and the things of this world.

*God, I know there is no way I can be spotless
and blameless on my own. I'm so thankful that
You see me as clean and pure because of Jesus.*

GRACE AND TRUTH

But grow in the grace and knowledge of our Lord and Savior
Jesus Christ. To him be glory both now and forever! Amen.
2 Peter 3:18 niv

* *

Think back to Grace's story. At her college "Bible study," she was learn-ing a lot about grace and her friends were really nice. But she wasn't learning about truth. That's why having both things is necessary.

And you can learn all there is to know about the Bible, but if you don't have love, it doesn't matter. Check it out: "If I have the gift of prophecy and can fathom all mysteries and all knowledge, and if I have a faith that can move mountains, but do not have love, I am nothing" (1 Corinthians 13:2 niv).

If you're full of knowledge and growing successfully in lots of ways but aren't living in love, you've accomplished nothing in the kingdom of God. If you're full of grace and love but aren't walking in truth, you're living a life of meaninglessness.

Let that sink in. Bring this issue to Jesus and ask Him to align your thoughts and your heart with His.

Jesus, please show me what it means to grow in
grace and truth with love covering my life.

WORDS FROM A FRIEND

We proclaim to you the one who existed from the beginning, whom we have heard and seen. We saw him with our own eyes and touched him with our own hands. He is the Word of life.

1 JOHN 1:1 NLT

Here we are in 1 John. John wrote this letter to believers to show how faith should affect a person's life. John was most likely the last surviving apostle when he wrote it. He was friends with Jesus and walked closely with Him. He followed Jesus, knew Him personally, and loved Him. John knew what he was talking about here, and we would all do well to listen.

Second Timothy 3:16 (NIV) says, "All Scripture is God-breathed and is useful for teaching, rebuking, correcting and training in righteousness," so we know that the book of 1 John was inspired by the Holy Spirit. As we spend some time here, ask the Holy Spirit to make these scriptures come alive in your heart and mind.

Lord, I'm thankful for Your Word. Let Your Holy Spirit rise up in me as I get to know You more through the book of 1 John.

LIGHT VS. DARK

This is the message we have heard from him and declare to you: God is light; in him there is no darkness at all.
1 JOHN 1:5 NIV

. . . .

God is light. The Amplified Bible helps us understand this a little better: "God is Light [He is holy, His message is truthful, He is perfect in righteousness], and in Him there is no darkness at all [no sin, no wickedness, no imperfection]."

Have you seen any of the *Star Wars* movies? These are epic movies that highlight the difference between good and evil, light and dark. We love cheering for the good guys to win, defeating the dark side.

God is holy and good and perfect in all His ways. And He's the only one who can lead you out of darkness.

Ask Jesus to shine His light on your heart. The psalmist prayed in Psalm 139:23–24 (NIV), "Search me, God, and know my heart; test me and know my anxious thoughts. See if there is any offensive way in me, and lead me in the way everlasting."

Lord, please shine Your light into my heart and mind. Spotlight anything that is getting in the way of my relationship with You. Lead me out of the dark and into Your light.

PRETENDING

If we claim to have fellowship with him and yet walk in the darkness, we lie and do not live out the truth. But if we walk in the light, as he is in the light, we have fellowship with one another, and the blood of Jesus, his Son, purifies us from all sin.
1 JOHN 1:6–7 NIV

Jana loved Bible quizzing when she was in high school. She enjoyed meeting new friends and hanging out with other Christian kids when they would get together for quiz rallies. There was this one boy she was particularly happy to see at the rallies every few months. Jana got to know this guy outside of Bible quizzing. Sadly, she learned that the "Bible stuff" wasn't real for him. He was good at Bible quizzing and acted the part of a Christian, but he didn't take any of it to heart. He was living another life when he wasn't at church.

The Bible is clear about pretending to be a Christian: it's a lie. Jesus calls us to walk in the light with Him where He purifies us from sin.

Lord, I want to walk in the light with You. Show me any way that I might be pretending and purify me. I pray for my friends who struggle with pretending too. Soften their hearts to hear and respond to Your truth.

CONFESSION

If we confess our sins, he is faithful and just and will forgive us our sins and purify us from all unrighteousness.
1 John 1:9 niv

- -

We all mess up. It's part of being human. Sometimes you might be tempted to hide from God when you sin. I mean, that's what Adam and Eve did, right? But God wants you to come to Him instead. Talk to Him about it. Turn back to Him and trust Him to be faithful to you.

The Amplified Bible explains that God "will forgive our sins and cleanse us continually from all unrighteousness [our wrongdoing, everything not in conformity with His will and purpose]."

There is something very powerful about coming to God and confessing your sins to Him. He wants to cleanse you "continually." He wants to help you through your situation and give you peace. He wants to remind you of who you really are to Him.

Jesus already paid the price for your sin—once and for all on the cross. Your salvation is secure. And when you come to Him again when you've messed up, you get to clear the air. Your relationship with God gets deeper and stronger.

Lord, thanks for being so faithful to me! I come to You with all my sin and ask that You would change me and restore our relationship.

165

HOW YOU KNOW

But if anyone obeys his word, love for God is truly made complete in them. This is how we know we are in him: Whoever claims to live in him must live as Jesus did.

1 John 2:5–6 niv

Back to Grace's story again. She was deceived by the enemy and by friends who used God's Word in ways that weren't true. You're going to come across this a lot as you grow up. The enemy will do to you what he did to Eve back in the garden. He'll try to get you to question everything you know about God. You'll hear things like "Did God really mean. . . ?" and "If God is love, how could. . . ?" and he'll plant some seeds of doubt in you.

It's good to find out what you believe and why. Go through God's Word and find out what He says about life and eternity and people and love. Ask for wisdom from older Christians.

But here's how you know if someone is following Jesus: they will love God and obey His Word. That's how to know who belongs to Him.

God, I want to obey Your Word. Teach me and lead me as I grow up. Keep me from being deceived by the enemy.

REMAIN IN HIM

Now, little children (believers, dear ones), remain in
Him [with unwavering faith], so that when He appears
[at His return], we may have [perfect] confidence and
not be ashamed and shrink away from Him at His coming.
1 John 2:28 amp

- -

In John 15:4 (NIV), Jesus said, "Remain in me, as I also remain in you. No branch can bear fruit by itself; it must remain in the vine. Neither can you bear fruit unless you remain in me."

My family has multiple fruit trees on our property. The peaches have been growing well the past few years. This spring, however, we noticed that only one branch of our peach tree has any leaves on it! The rest of the branches are dead. Insects or disease could have caused their demise. The only chance our tree has of survival is if we cut off all the diseased and dead branches. Then, just maybe, the branch that remains will thrive again.

Similarly, we must remain in Jesus and get rid of any diseased branches in our lives if we want to be fruitful and have victory over the enemy.

Jesus, You have my heart. Give me the desire to remain
in You so that I can thrive in this life You've given me.

GOD'S CORRECTION

*See what great love the Father has lavished
on us, that we should be called children
of God! And that is what we are!*
1 JOHN 3:1 NIV

Our great God is a good Father. The very best. You may struggle with the way you were parented, but God parents perfectly. He always welcomes you with love and grace, even when you've made a mistake. He lavishes you with His love because you're His child. His correction is clear and kind; His discipline is loving and hope filled. He won't shame you.

The Bible tells us in Romans 2:4 that it is God's loving-kindness that brings us to repentance. Hebrews 12:8–10 (MSG) helps us understand this better: "Only irresponsible parents leave children to fend for themselves. Would you prefer an irresponsible God? We respect our own parents for training and not spoiling us, so why not embrace God's training so we can truly live? While we were children, our parents did what seemed best to them. But God is doing what is best for us, training us to live God's holy best."

*Thank You for parenting me perfectly, Father God.
I'm thankful that You care about the choices I make in life.
Thank You for seeing me and setting me on the right path.*

I'M ALL YOURS

Dear friends, we are already God's children, but he has not yet shown us what we will be like when Christ appears. But we do know that we will be like him, for we will see him as he really is. And all who have this eager expectation will keep themselves pure, just as he is pure.
1 JOHN 3:2–3 NLT

Can you imagine actually seeing Jesus face-to-face for the first time? This might actually happen in your lifetime! The Bible tells us amazing things that will happen to us in the end times. While we wait for Jesus to return, God wants us to be pure like He is. But remember, we can't do this on our own.

The Bible says that if you are a follower of Jesus, you are being transformed into His likeness day by day (2 Corinthians 3:17–18). His Spirit invades your life and changes you, keeping you pure for what is to come.

Jesus, thank You for Your Spirit, who is always at work in my heart. Thank You that I don't have to be afraid or worried that I have to become pure all on my own. I'm Yours, Jesus!

LED ASTRAY

Dear children, do not let anyone lead you astray.
1 JOHN 3:7 NIV

. . . .

The Message paraphrases 1 John 3:7–8 like this: "So, my dear children, don't let anyone divert you from the truth. It's the person who acts right who is right, just as we see it lived out in our righteous Messiah. Those who make a practice of sin are straight from the Devil, the pioneer in the practice of sin. The Son of God entered the scene to abolish the Devil's ways."

Sometimes sin isn't easy to spot, right? The enemy can be very sneaky. That's called "insidious evil," evil that's right in your face but you can't even see it. A good example is Rapunzel's mom. She kept her hidden away for her own selfish reasons, all the while pretending to love Rapunzel and be her mother.

That's a fairy tale, but it happens all the time in the real world. People say they are Christians, but they are selfish and dark on the inside. So how do you keep from being led astray? You stay close to Jesus. His Spirit, who is at work in you, will tell you right from wrong. If you are listening for Him in your life every day, you'll hear Him speaking.

Jesus, please continue to speak to me.
I want to stay close to You.

REAL LOVE

This is how we know what love is: Jesus Christ
laid down his life for us. And we ought to lay
down our lives for our brothers and sisters.
1 JOHN 3:16 NIV

Get ready for the gross factor. (You've been warned!) A young mom was wiping off the wall where her infant son had smeared his diaper (told ya!). It really was disgusting. But she realized in that moment that love was not a feeling. It was a choice and an action. She cleaned up after her son, not because she felt like it—she certainly didn't; she was exhausted!—but because she loved her son.

This mom never knew what real love was until she had a child of her own. Then it made sense. Jesus didn't love her because she deserved love or because He just felt like it. He chose to love her and He acted on it. He laid down His life for hers. He does the same for you and me.

Jesus, You alone show me what real love is.
Help me not to be swayed by my feelings
but to stand on the truth of Your love.

A THOUSAND WORDS

*Dear children, let's not merely say that we love
each other; let us show the truth by our actions.*
1 JOHN 3:18 NLT

- -

Have you heard the saying "A picture is worth a thousand words"? Think about that for a minute. You could go on an amazing trip to another country and try to tell your friends about it over the phone, but no amount of words could help you explain the beauty. But a picture might! The picture still might not capture all the details, but it works a lot better than words sometimes.

That's a bit like this verse. You can say you love someone for years and years. But until you show them with your actions, the words don't mean much. Take chores, for example. Does anyone actually like them? Not really, but you do them because you are part of a family and you love your parents. Doing chores with a happy heart is one way to show your love.

What are some other ways you can show your love for someone with your actions? Talk to Jesus about this.

*Lord, help me love with my whole heart.
And help me show it with my actions.*

CHILL OUT

*If our hearts condemn us, we know that God is
greater than our hearts, and he knows everything.*
1 JOHN 3:20 NIV

· ·

Remember how I said looking at several different Bible translations can be helpful? Let's take a look at this verse in a few different translations and paraphrases and see what we learn:

Amplified Bible: "For God is greater than our heart and He knows all things [nothing is hidden from Him because we are in His hands]."

The Message: "For God is greater than our worried hearts and knows more about us than we do ourselves."

New Life Version: "Our heart may say that we have done wrong. But remember, God is greater than our heart. He knows everything."

New Living Translation: "Even if we feel guilty, God is greater than our feelings, and he knows everything."

One Bible commentary suggests that John was talking to people who were worried that they weren't doing enough for Jesus. And this verse is a reminder that God knows our hearts better than we know ourselves. So chill out. God will lead you to do what He wants you to as long as you're listening for His voice and obeying Him.

*Lord, You know my heart. I want to listen and obey. Lead me
to do what's right, and help me to leave my worries behind!*

GOD'S FAVORITE

And this is his commandment: We must believe in the name of his Son, Jesus Christ, and love one another, just as he commanded us. Those who obey God's commandments remain in fellowship with him, and he with them. And we know he lives in us because the Spirit he gave us lives in us.
1 JOHN 3:23–24 NLT

. . . .

John was known as the disciple "Jesus loved." This never made sense to me (because didn't Jesus love all the disciples?) until I met Grammy B. She loved God deeply. And she was fond of often saying, "God loves you, but I'm His favorite." She had such a deep relationship with God that she felt like God's favorite daughter.

John wrote the books of 1 John and the Gospel of John. In John 13:23 (NIV), John wrote, "One of them, the disciple whom Jesus loved, was reclining next to him." If Grammy B had been writing a book, that's what she'd write too. God's love can make you feel like you're the only one in the world.

And that unmatched love pours out of us to everyone around us because of God's Spirit, who lives in us.

Lord, Your love is one of a kind.
Thanks for pouring Your love into me.

LOOK IT UP!

Dear friends, do not believe everyone who claims to speak by the Spirit. You must test them to see if the spirit they have comes from God. For there are many false prophets in the world.
1 JOHN 4:1 NLT

* *

The Message paraphrases this verse, "Don't believe everything you hear. Carefully weigh and examine what people tell you. Not everyone who talks about God comes from God. There are a lot of lying preachers loose in the world."

Remember that the enemy likes to trick people. And he's really good at it. He likes to deceive, and the Bible says that he even disguises himself as an angel of light (2 Corinthians 11:14).

Often people who have been deceived like to take certain verses out of the Bible and use them to say what they want them to say. So always test what people say about God with His Word. Look it up. Find a study Bible or an online study Bible and find out what God's Word really says.

You have the Spirit of God right there in your heart, so if someone says something about God and it doesn't feel right, check it out.

God, please give me wisdom about You.
Thank You that I have Your Spirit to guide me.

JESUS IS GREATER

Little children, you are from God and have overcome them,
for he who is in you is greater than he who is in the world.
1 JOHN 4:4 ESV

Do you have a certain fear that you struggle with on a regular basis? Maybe it's getting up in front of people. Maybe you struggle with nightmares or being alone in the dark.

Philippians 2:10 (NIV) says, "At the name of Jesus every knee should bow, in heaven and on earth and under the earth." Jesus is always bigger than anything you fear.

If you are in the middle of a situation that is causing you to be afraid, sometimes simply saying the name of Jesus in faith is the best prayer you can pray. When you call on Jesus' name, you're asking Him to take your fears and fill you with His love and peace instead. Darkness has to leave when Jesus enters. Memorizing 1 John 4:4 (ESV) is a great one for the Holy Spirit to bring to mind too: "He who is in you is greater than he who is in the world."

Jesus, I trust that there is power in Your name.
Thank You for rescuing me from fear.

CHOOSING LOVE

Dear friends, let us continue to love one another, for love comes from God. Anyone who loves is a child of God and knows God.
1 JOHN 4:7 NLT

• •

John really wanted brothers and sisters in Christ to love one another. He told them over and over again to love one another. If love came easy, why would we need so many reminders? Because love isn't a feeling.

Movies and TV shows and social media may present love as a feeling you get when you're around "the one." That's not real love. That's being "in" love. But that feeling comes and goes depending on the circumstances and the other person's response to you. People fall out of love all the time. That's why the divorce rate is so high in the world.

Agape love is different. It's love from God that lasts forever. It's making a choice to love another person even when you don't feel like it. You can show agape love to everyone around you. You can choose love and let your actions tell the truth about your words. This shows a watching world the true love of God.

God, please fill me with Your love and strength
to love even when my feelings tell me otherwise.

COME ALIVE

*This is how God showed his love among us: He sent his one
and only Son into the world that we might live through him.
This is love: not that we loved God, but that he loved us and
sent his Son as an atoning sacrifice for our sins. Dear friends,
since God so loved us, we also ought to love one another.*

1 John 4:9–11 niv

Jesus came for you so that you might come alive through Him. In Luke 4:18–19 (NIV), Jesus said, "The Spirit of the Lord is on me, because he has anointed me to proclaim good news to the poor. He has sent me to proclaim freedom for the prisoners and recovery of sight for the blind, to set the oppressed free, to proclaim the year of the Lord's favor."

He was not just talking about poor people and prisoners. These words from Jesus are for you! Jesus came to bring you healing and freedom from sin and death. He also came to bring you abundant life through Him that starts right now (John 10:10).

Life can be hard, but you are never alone. Jesus is with you, carrying your burdens and breathing new life into you in each moment.

Jesus, breathe new life into me this day as I follow You.

GOD AT WORK

No one has ever seen God. But if we love each other,
God lives in us, and his love is brought to full
expression in us. And God has given us his Spirit
as proof that we live in him and he in us.
1 JOHN 4:12–13 NLT

One day we'll be able to see Jesus face-to-face. That's the promise we have as God's children. But for now, the Bible tells us that we see God by seeing His Spirit alive and at work in us and in believers around us. God is love. And when you see love in action, you are seeing God at work.

We also see evidence of God in all of His creation. God can speak to us in many ways. He is the master artist. He paints us a new picture with every sunrise and sunset. Do you see God at work around you? Journal some of the ways you've seen Him work as part of your prayer today.

Thank You for Your amazing creation that speaks
to me every day, God! Help me love others well
so that they can see You at work in me.

LOVING GOD

And so we know and rely on the love God has for us. God is love. Whoever lives in love lives in God, and God in them.
1 John 4:16 niv

Do you ever wonder if you're loving God well? Do you find it sometimes difficult to say, "I love You, God," and wonder if you really mean it?

Sometimes it's hard to know how to love God back after He sacrificed everything for you. His great love can be overwhelming! But when we obey God's Word, listen for His voice, and love others, that is how we show love to God.

And when those times come when you aren't sure that you are loving God very well? Today's verse answers that question: "We know and rely on the love God has for us." The only way we can love at all is because He loved us first. He is the author of love, and He'll continue to show us how to love better and better as we follow Him.

Lord God, please help me to listen for Your voice in my life and to follow after You, relying on the love You have for me.

NO FEAR IN LOVE

There is no fear in love. But perfect love drives out fear, because fear has to do with punishment. The one who fears is not made perfect in love. We love because he first loved us.

1 John 4:18–19 niv

The biggest blessing in your life is that you have access to God. You can always approach Him without fear because He sees you through the love and sacrifice of Jesus. Jesus made a way once and for all. So God is not angry with you. A person who is afraid of God's punishment doesn't understand who they are in Christ. He is a good Father, longing to hold you and love you well all the days of your life.

You don't have to work harder or be a better Christian to earn God's love. When you begin to believe who you are in Christ, it changes everything. You start living differently. You realize how deeply loved you are, and that sets you free. Remember this: as Jesus pours His love and His Spirit into your life, it spills over into the lives of those around you.

Thank You, God, that I'm able to come to You without fear because of Jesus!

BORN OF GOD

Everyone who believes that Jesus is the Christ has been born of God, and everyone who loves the Father loves whoever has been born of him.

1 JOHN 5:1 ESV

The Bible says in several places that you are "born of God." First John 5:18 (NIV) says, "We know that anyone born of God does not continue to sin; the One who was born of God keeps them safe, and the evil one cannot harm them."

So what does "born of God" mean? The Amplified Bible explains that being born of God means "a divine and supernatural birth— they are born of God—spiritually transformed, renewed, sanctified" (John 1:13).

This supernatural truth is more binding than your physical reality. It's eternal! In Christ, you are God's child with rights to His full inheritance. You are born into His family. He keeps you safe, He frees you from slavery to sin so you don't have to go back to it again and again, and the evil one is not permitted to destroy you. Are you walking in this truth? Keep your chin up! You are chosen by God and kept safe in His love for eternity.

Lord, I choose to believe Your Word. I'm Your child. I will live with gratitude in my heart for all You've done.

NOT A BURDEN

Loving God means keeping his commandments,
and his commandments are not burdensome.
1 JOHN 5:3 NLT

- -

Ella was a new Christian looking for a church home. She was praying for God to lead her to the right one. Something was wrong at one of them. The people didn't seem joyful. Church was a solemn experience. At another church, the pastor talked mostly about suffering for Jesus like soldiers exhausting themselves in battle until they got to heaven where life would finally be good. But she had some questions about that. Yes, she understood that life would be hard and that sometimes suffering was needed. But didn't Jesus promise abundant life too?

Ella moved along to another church. The pastor preached on Matthew 11:28–30 (NIV). As he was reading scripture, Ella heard Jesus saying these words directly to her heart: "Come to me, all you who are weary and burdened, and I will give you rest. Take my yoke upon you and learn from me, for I am gentle and humble in heart, and you will find rest for your souls. For my yoke is easy and my burden is light."

Ella learned that God Himself gives us strength to keep His commandments. As we come to Jesus in every moment, He carries our burdens and gives us rest.

Jesus, I am excited and thankful for the
abundant life that we get to live together!

ASK FOR ANYTHING

This is the confidence we have in approaching God:
that if we ask anything according to his will, he hears us.
And if we know that he hears us—whatever we ask—
we know that we have what we asked of him.
1 John 5:14–15 niv

Our family had the opportunity to move across the country. We weren't sure if this is what God wanted for us, so we began to pray as a family for every little detail. We believed that nothing was too big or too small for God to speak to us about. After all, James 4:2 (NIV) says, "You do not have because you do not ask God." So we started asking. We had an actual list.

We brought our list before God, and He began to answer every single question on the list. It was amazing to watch Him work as the four of us came to Him in prayer multiple times a day. We had a need that would arise during the move, and an email would show up with the answer. The inspection fell through; God had another one set up. It was awesome!

The key here is that when we ask God, according to His will, He says, "Yes!" He obviously wanted us to move because He said yes to every one of our questions.

Lord, I want Your will in my life!
Thanks for hearing my prayers!

LIVING IN FELLOWSHIP WITH GOD

And we know that the Son of God has come, and he has given us understanding so that we can know the true God. And now we live in fellowship with the true God because we live in fellowship with his Son, Jesus Christ. He is the only true God, and he is eternal life.
1 JOHN 5:20 NLT

The Bible makes it clear that God has made Himself known to us through His creation. Signs of God are everywhere. Miracles are everywhere. We are without excuse when it comes to believing that intelligent design is behind every natural wonder.

Jesus Christ is the one true God. He proved it by coming alive after He was put to death. Everything He ever said was and is true. Isaiah 42:5–6 (NLT) says, "God, the LORD, created the heavens and stretched them out. He created the earth and everything in it. He gives breath to everyone, life to everyone who walks the earth. And it is he who says, 'I, the LORD, have called you to demonstrate my righteousness. I will take you by the hand and guard you.' "

Jesus, my one true God, I'm amazed that You want to take me by the hand and guide me forever. Thank You for giving me eternal life!

185

THE GREATEST COMMAND

Jesus replied: " 'Love the Lord your God with all your
heart and with all your soul and with all your mind.'
This is the first and greatest commandment. And the
second is like it: 'Love your neighbor as yourself.' "
MATTHEW 22:37–39 NIV

As we end our time together, here's the most important scripture to remember: love God, and love your neighbor as yourself. There is a hidden truth in this scripture that most people ignore. Many people hear this passage and think, *Love God and love others. The end.* But Jesus said to "love your neighbor as yourself." And what does "as yourself" have to do with anything? This is the mention of your identity. "Yourself" is about who you truly are in Christ. Pastor Robert Gelinas of Colorado Community Church in Aurora, Colorado, says that God wants you to see yourself the way He sees you. And then you can love others out of that truth.

Bottom line? Love God. Love others as yourself. See yourself the way God sees you:

Loved.

Chosen.

Lord, thank You for all that You've taught me over
the past few months. Thank You for choosing me!
Help me to see myself as You see me and to live
out this greatest commandment in Your strength.

SCRIPTURE INDEX

OLD TESTAMENT

GENESIS
1:27...........................68

EXODUS
15:20 39

DEUTERONOMY
30:19 120
33:27 52

JUDGES
4:4–5 37

RUTH
1:16..........................42

1 SAMUEL
2:1–2 45

1 CHRONICLES
16:23–24 54

ESTHER
4:14..........................38

PSALMS
3:3............................88
16:11 56
18:19 104

30:2....................... 128
34:17 87
37:23–24 111
46:1–2 80
50:9–10.....................15
86:8–10.....................71
100:1–3.................. 119
103:2 90
119:105.................. 115
121:8 110
147:11.................... 113
149:4 85

PROVERBS
3:7–8 126
11:14 129
14:30 121
24:16 131

ISAIAH
25:1........................ 117
26:3........................ 132
30:21 98
40:11 102
40:13–14 108
41:10 112

43:6–7 114
53:5 125
59:17 26

JEREMIAH
1:5 20
10:12–13 69
17:14 118
31:3 99

JOEL
2:12–13 116
2:28 97

NEW TESTAMENT

MATTHEW
6:14–15 .51
9:37–38 .55
19:26 65
22:37–39 186
25:34–36 53
28:20 96

MARK
5:34 127
10:45 50
16:9 47

LUKE
1:38 43

1:41–42 .44
2:38 46
15:20 14
22:31–32 94

JOHN
1:12 17
3:16 35
4:13–14 100
4:28–30 49
6:37 84
8:32 105
13:34–35 18
14:2–3 67
15:15 86
15:16 21
17:17 107
17:20–21 91

ACTS
1:8 109
16:14 40

ROMANS
5:8 83
6:6 61
8:16–17 13
8:17 76
12:1 11
12:4–5 95

12:10 103	4:29. 63
15:7. 130	6:13. . . . . 24, 25
15:13 64	**COLOSSIANS**
16:3. 41	1:13–14. 60
1 CORINTHIANS	3:3. 101
1:2–3 58	3:16. 78
7:17. 66	**1 THESSALONIANS**
10:13 28	5:11. 75
12:27 57	**2 THESSALONIANS**
13:4–7 19	3:3. 73
2 CORINTHIANS	**2 TIMOTHY**
1:20. 133	1:5. 48
6:8. 70	2:11–12. 9
GALATIANS	3:16–17. 27
1:15–16. 16	**TITUS**
3:28–29. 36	2:11–12. 62
4:5–6 12	**HEBREWS**
6:7. 72	4:12. 106
EPHESIANS	4:16. 8
1:3–4 7	7:25. 93
1:13–14. 59	10:24–25 74
3:12. 30	**JAMES**
3:14–17. 31	1:5. 23
3:17–18. 32	1:18. 89
3:19. 33	3:13. 123
3:20–21. 34	

4:7. 29
4:8. 124

1 PETER
1:1. 134
1:2. 135
1:3–4 136
1:5. 137
1:6–7 138
1:13–15. 139
1:17–19. 140
2:1–3 141
2:9. 10
2:10. 142
2:16. 143
2:24. 144
3:3–4 145
3:8–9 79
3:10–12. 146
3:15–16. 147
4:7–8 148
4:8–10 .77
4:10–11. 149
4:12–13. 150
5:5. 122
5:6. 151
5:7. 152
5:8–9 153

2 PETER
1:3. 154
1:5–7 155
1:16. 156
2:1–2 157
2:21. 158
3:9. 159
3:14. 160
3:18. 161

1 JOHN
1:1. 162
1:5. 163
1:6–7 164
1:9. 165
2:1. 92
2:5–6 166
2:15–16. 22
2:28. 167
3:1. 168
3:2–3 169
3:7. 170
3:16. 171
3:18. 172
3:20. 173
3:23–24. 174
4:1. 175
4:4. 176

4:7 177
4:9–11 178
4:10 82
4:12–13 179
4:16 . . . . 81, 180
4:18–19 181
5:1 182
5:3 183
5:14–15 184
5:20 185

MORE ENCOURAGEMENT FOR YOUR BEAUTIFUL SPIRIT!

You Belong
Devotions and Prayers for a Teen Girl's Heart

**You Were Created with Purpose by a Loving,
Heavenly Creator. . .You Belong!**

This delightful devotional is a lovely reminder that you were created with purpose by a heavenly Creator. . .and that you belong—right here and now—in this world. 180 encouraging readings and inspiring prayers, rooted in biblical truth, will reassure your uncertain heart, helping you to understand that you're *never* alone and *always* loved. In each devotional reading, you will encounter the bountiful blessings and grace of your Creator, while coming to trust His purposeful plan for you in this world.

Flexible Casebound / 978-1-63609-169-3